ᬦᬋᬮᬜ᭄ᬘᬾᬭᬤ᭄᭙ᬕᬢᬶ॥᭘᭙॥

ᬓᭀᬗᬤᬘᬶᬭᬫᬋ॥᭙᭒॥

ᬓᬘᭀᬢᬭᬤᬘᬶᬭᬤᬶᬜᬶ॥᭙᭑॥

ᬮ᭄ᬭᬓᬘᬤᬶᬧᬸᬮᬭ॥᭑॥

ᬅᬩᬶᬘᭂᬢᬶᬩᬥᬳᬤᬶᬲᬾ॥

ᬓᬭᬷᬧᬓᬘᬢᬶᬧᬸᬮᬭ॥᭔॥

ᬦᬢᬘᬶᬬᬘᬾᬧᬸ᭄ᬮᬭᬶᬯᬶᬲᬸᬩᬘᬶᬦ

ᬦᬢᬭᬓᬶᬓᬢᬸᬳᬢᬭᬶᬳᬅ᭄ᬭᬸᬓᬶ

ᬅᬷ᬴᭄ᬚᬸᬫᬘᬾᬫᬲᬶᬧᬸᬯᬶ᭙॥

Myanmar Style

Art, Architecture and Design of Burma

Myanmar Style

Art, Architecture and Design of Burma

John Falconer • Elizabeth Moore • Daniel Kahrs • Alfred Birnbaum • Virginia McKeen Di Crocco • Joe Cummings

Photography by Luca Invernizzi Tettoni

Thames and Hudson

British Library Cataloguing-in-Publication Data
A catalogue record for this book is available from the British Library

ISBN 0-500-01890-1
Printed in Singapore

Editor's Note:
For many towns and areas, there are a number of different Burmese place names. The most obvious are Myanmar/Burma, Yangon/Rangoon, Bagan/Pagan—but there are many more. Our intention in this book has been to use the correct name for a place in its correct historical context. Whenever clarification is needed, we have inserted the alternative name(s). Because some of the "new" names are not known to the average reader (for example "Ayeraywady" is the new spelling of "Irrawaddy"), in these cases "old" names are retained for clarification purposes.

A Note from the Photographer:
Over many years of travelling in the country, I have learned that this is not only home to the most intriguing culture in Asia, but also home to some of the most hospitable people on earth. Furthermore, it is an extremely safe country to travel within. Nowhere else have I found so many people ready to help me without question, so many people ready to open the doors of their houses without knowing who I was or what I was doing.

Many people have helped and supported me on this project. Certainly I would not have been able to produce this book without the help—in particular—of Daniel Kahrs, Christopher Burt and Patrick and Claudia Robert. In Bangkok, Khun Anong Ulapathorn of Rama Art has always supported my projects, and remains a great friend. Thanks also to Peng Seng Antiques and Galerie d'Art. In Singapore, Edmund and Angela Koh of Lopburi Art and Antiques have put their collection at my disposal and offered invaluable help and advice. Darika Suter of Eastern Discoveries has also contributed some beautiful pieces to the selection photographed in the book. In Myanmar, I want to thank my guide and travelling companion, Kyaw Swar Htoon, the comedian Lu Maw of Moustache Brothers, U Aung Nyunt, Min Min Aung, Tin Win of Beikthano Gallery, Jürgen Voss, Juergen Von Jordan, Myint Myint Sein, and Olivier Vayasset. Cherie Aung-Khin, her husband Sunny, the staff of the Elephant House and the "Commander" have also provided many objects for photography and given me every assistance.

င်းကနက် မြတ် ရှိဘုရားကိုဆွမ်းတော်ကြီးကတားမဲ့

Contents

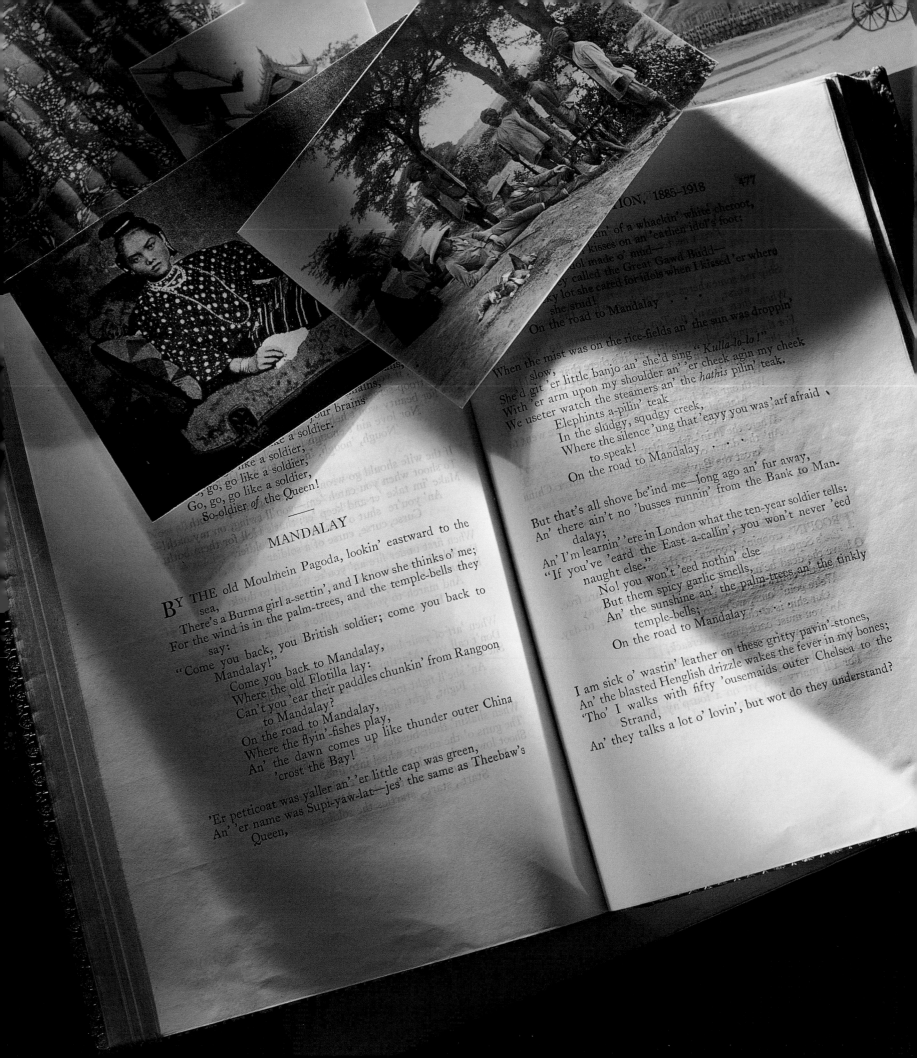

MANDALAY

BY THE old Moulmein Pagoda, lookin' eastward to the sea,
There's a Burma girl a-settin', and I know she thinks o' me;
For the wind is in the palm-trees, and the temple-bells they say:
"Come you back, you British soldier; come you back to Mandalay!"
    Come you back to Mandalay,
    Where the old Flotilla lay:
    Can't you 'ear their paddles chunkin' from Rangoon to Mandalay?
        On the road to Mandalay,
        Where the flyin'-fishes play,
        An' the dawn comes up like thunder outer China 'crost the Bay!

'Er petticoat was yaller an' 'er little cap was green,
An' 'er name was Supi-yaw-lat—jes' the same as Theebaw's Queen,

...un' of a whackin' white cheroot,
...kisses on an 'eathen idol's foot;
...ol made o' mud—
...y called the Great Gawd Budd—
...y lot she cared for idols when I kissed 'er where she stud!
    On the road to Mandalay . . . . .

When the mist was on the rice-fields an' the sun was droppin' slow,
She'd git 'er little banjo an' she'd sing "Kulla-lo-lo!"
With 'er arm upon my shoulder an' 'er cheek agin my cheek
We useter watch the steamers an' the *hathis* pilin' teak.
    Elephints a-pilin' teak
    In the sludgy, squdgy creek,
    Where the silence 'ung that 'eavy you was 'arf afraid to speak!
        On the road to Mandalay . . . . .

But that's all shove be'ind me—long ago an' fur away,
An' there ain't no 'busses runnin' from the Bank to Mandalay;
An' I'm learnin' 'ere in London what the ten-year soldier tells:
"If you've 'eard the East a-callin', you won't never 'eed naught else."
    No! you won't 'eed nothin' else
    But them spicy garlic smells,
    An' the sunshine an' the palm-trees an' the tinkly temple-bells;
        On the road to Mandalay . . . . .

I am sick o' wastin' leather on these gritty pavin'-stones,
An' the blasted Henglish drizzle wakes the fever in my bones;
'Tho' I walks with fifty 'ousemaids outer Chelsea to the Strand,
An' they talks a lot o' lovin', but wot do they understand?

Introduction

"By the old Moulmein Pagoda, lookin' lazy at the sea,
There's a Burma girl a-settin', and I know she thinks o' me;
For the wind is in the palm-trees, and the temple-bells they say:
'Come you back, you British soldier; come you back to Mandalay!'"

The lament of Kipling's private soldier, dreaming of the east in the cold and dankness of "the blasted English drizzle" evokes the charm of an eastern dream, a now unattainable fantasy to a demobbed soldier on the wet streets of London. The most popular of Kipling's ballads, the mood of 'The Road to Mandalay' mingled jingoistic pride in the British conquest of Burma (Myanmar), with a melancholy yearning for the colours and sounds of the east. This nostalgia-fuelled fantasy conjured an exquisite dream of oriental languor and beauty—the clang of temple bells, misty rice fields, the whiff of spices and the tender ministrations of cigar-smoking Burmese maidens "in a cleaner, greener land". For the common soldier tramping the dirty London streets and dreaming of "long ago an' fur away", Mandalay is the key to a land of stronger colour, intenser smells and, of course, erotic opportunity ("plucky lot she cared for idols when I kissed her where she stud!"), a broadening of experience and a shrugging off of restraint, "somewheres east of Suez...where there ain't no Ten Commandments an' a man can raise a thirst".

Rudyard Kipling's road to Mandalay was of course the great waterway of the Irrawaddy which carried invading British forces from Rangoon (present-day Yangon) to the heart of the Burmese kingdom in 1885. The vision, though, is shot through with irony, as the annexation of Upper Burma, which opened up the country to the west, inevitably undermined many of those aspects of the old Burma so attractive to Kipling and those who followed in his footsteps. But the greater irony of Kipling's poem lies in the very shortness of his own stay in the country: far from travelling up the Irrawaddy with the "old flotilla", Kipling's personal knowledge of the country was a one-day stop at Rangoon in March 1888 and a brief visit to Moulmein (Mawalamyine) across the Gulf of Martaban to the east, where the great pagoda inspired the ballad's most famous lines. But no matter that Moulmein lies far from the road to Mandalay, the sacrifice of topographical exactitude for poetic effect has fuelled the fantasies of many a traveller from the 19th century to the present day, for whom the lure of the river highway into the heart of Burma encompasses all the romance of an exotic tropical world.

 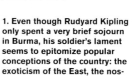

1. Even though Rudyard Kipling only spent a very brief sojourn in Burma, his soldier's lament seems to epitomize popular conceptions of the country: the exoticism of the East, the nostalgia for better times and more than a hint of potential amorous conquest.
2. 'A Girl Painting her Eyebrows', from a painting by J Raeburn Middleton *circa* 1900. V C Scott O'Connor wrote in his seminal guidebook to Burma, *The Silken*

***East* (1903): "When she is young the Burmese woman is, after her own type, fair and attractive, full of laughter and fun and the enjoyment of life; witty and self-possessed; seldom if ever brazen-faced; frank to a degree. It is one of the wayside amusements of travel in Burma to see her at her toilette before the world, to see her calmly unwind tresses in her hair (itself generally luxurious and ample); to see her enamel her face with ingenuous *thanaka*, to follow her frequent contented glances at her mirror." Much taken with both the men and women of the country, O'Connor's description of Burmese maidenhood evokes his deep admiration for the country's fairer sex.**

While Portuguese and Italian merchants were the first Europeans to visit Burma as early as the mid-15th century, the British connection with the country dated back to almost exactly 300 years before the annexation. In 1586 the merchant Edward Fitch spent nearly a year in the country, looking for trading opportunities, gathering information and marvelling at the capital at Pegu (Bago), "a very great citie, strong and fair" and at that time larger than London. For the next two and a half centuries Britain maintained a precarious commercial foothold, first at Syriam (near the present site of Yangon), from where they were expelled in 1752 and later at Cape Negrais on the southernmost tip of the Arakan peninsula, whose garrison was destroyed by King Alaungpaya seven years later. The massacre of the Negrais factory virtually ended British contacts until the early 19th century. Then the activities of an increasingly expansionist and aggressive Burma under King Bagyidaw led to war with Britain in 1824–26, resulting in the annexation of the southern coastal provinces of Arakan (Rakhine) and Tennasserim (Taninthayi). A second war in 1852 saw the loss of the whole of Pegu and Lower Burma to Britain.

With these territorial gains and the rapid expansion of Rangoon as a port in the following decades, British commercial interests were soon looking longingly to the riches of Upper Burma (as the old Kingdom of Ava was known to Europeans). The commercial and political stranglehold tightened, and with the death of King Mindon (whose relationship with the British had been friendly, if distant) and the accession of King Thibaw in 1878, informed observers saw the acquisition of the Kingdom of Ava and the dissolution of the Konbaung Dynasty as inevitable. Hopelessly dominated by his cruel and capricious wife Queen Supyalat, Thibaw's relations with the British were immediately brought to crisis point by the execution of some 80 of the King's relatives in 1879; and for a further six years they simmered uneasily as the rapacity of Queen Supyalat and her corrupt inner circle dragged the kingdom towards chaos. Thibaw's diplomatic flirtations with the French, a long-running border dispute with the British and increasing agitation for annexation from the Rangoon merchants all kept the pot boiling, until in 1885 Thibaw's commercial dispute with the Bombay-Burmah Trading Company over teak exports provided a pretext for invasion. In November the steamers of the Irrawaddy Flotilla Company started to ferry British troops up the Irrawaddy to Mandalay, at the start of a short campaign that saw Thibaw and his queen exiled in India and the last vestiges of the Burmese empire absorbed into Britain's Indian empire.

Thibaw's fall, which saw the extinction of an independent Burma for over half a century, was the dissolution of only the last of the dynasties which had risen to greatness and subsided along the banks of the Irrawaddy. The story of Burma for 1,000 years preceding British conquest was largely dominated by conflict between the settled Mons of Lower Burma and Burman invaders from the north; and while the creation of a unified Burma resulted from successive defeats of the Mons, it was their culture and influence—particularly the introduction of Buddhism—which was to be a defining element of Burmese culture. The first and greatest of the early kingdoms was the state of Pagan (Bagan), founded in the mid-9th century. Here, bounded at its western edge by the curving sweep of the Irrawaddy, a great city of temples stretches across the plain, witness to a vital architectural and artistic tradition, and material testament to a Buddhist polity centred on the merit-path to salvation. Pagan survived as a powerful kingdom for over four centuries, only falling to the Mongols and Shans at the end of the 13th century. While many of the temples have succumbed to decay, Pagan remains one of the world's great architectural sites. Barely known to outsiders before the mid-19th century, it excited the admiration of early European visitors unprepared for the elegance of a distinctive architectural heritage which reached its apogee in the 12th-century Ananda temple.

Other sites clustered along the banks of the river tell the story of succeeding dynasties, although the Burmese fondness for shifting capitals has led to a bewildering series of royal centres, much of whose abandoned magnificence is now lost. Little remains at Shwebo, where Alaungpaya, founder of the Konbaung Dynasty, ruled from 1750–60, or at Ava, which served as capital several times between the 14th and 18th centuries. And if few vestiges remain of the magnificence of Amarapura, selected as King Bodawpaya's capital in 1783, imaginative recreation is aided by the descriptions, paintings and photographs of the British officials who penetrated the secretive Burmese empire before annexation. Together, the remaining sites and documentary evidence paint a picture of a distinctive cultural style, whose predominantly brick and stucco architecture looks both towards India and Southeast Asia while remaining entirely individual.

Less concerned with leisurely sightseeing than later tourists, these officials nevertheless compiled exhaustive reports on the country. And if the tangible results of such missions were generally negligible (in 1795, Michael Symes, after a six weeks' journey up the Irrawaddy from Rangoon to Amarapura, was kept waiting four months before a brief audience at the royal court, at which he was merely observed in mildly curious silence for a few minutes before being ushered out of the royal presence), they provided valuable opportunities for gathering information. Thus, the mission which the governor-general of India sent

1. **Willoughby Wallace Hooper** took this photograph of the Hampshire Regiment soon after the occupation of Mandalay. It depicts the Church service on Christmas Day in 1885. He commented, "The Regiment is quartered in some of the numerous Phoongyee Kyoungs, or monasteries, outside the city walls on the N E. These buildings make capital barracks for the men.... The service on this day...was held in the open air outside one of these buildings...the men being paraded fully armed, as in those days it was impossible for any to say when an alarm might be sounded. This, as well as other buildings of the kind, was erected as 'a work of merit', but the builders little thought that one day the Christmas Hymn, 'Hark! The Herald Angels', would be sung by British soldiers in that place."
2. King Thibaw, Queen Supyalat and her sister in Mandalay Palace, 1880s. Western fascination with Burma was reciprocated by the Burmese royal family, who sent abroad for all manner of fashionable European toys. Photography was a particular favourite and for some years Thibaw kept a court photographer, a Frenchman with a staff of Burmese assistants. This photograph is from a negative found in the Palace after the British occupation. One of the Burmese assistants confirmed that the job had been profitable, if precarious: 'He was a very poor operator, and said that when he took a picture of the King, or more particularly when he took one of Queen Soopy-a-lat, it was an even chance whether he got a handful of rubies given to him or had his head cut off! The Frenchman gave up the situation.' Note the studio backdrop propped carelessly in the background.
3. 'The Begging Recluse', from a painting by J Raeburn Middleton. The giving of alms is a much-practised form of merit-making in Burma both past and present. As A W Wills wrote in *Sunny Days in Burma* (1905): "One of the precepts of the Buddha to his disciples was 'Let your daily food be broken victuals given to you as alms', and in obedience to this order one sees any morning, when one is astir early, little processions of monks and their pupils, each bearing a bowl-shaped vessel with a lid to it; as they wend their way slowly and in silence along the roads, they will stop at intervals before each cottage which they have to pass, and stand opposite to it with downcast eyes. Then one of its inmates will come forward and drop into the 'begging-bowl' a contribution of rice, a portion of curry, a bunch of vegetables, or some fruit. Not a word is said, and the procession moves on to the next dwelling.... The food which has been collected in the morning round, now serves to supply the wants of the brethren of the monastery...and of any wayfarers who may avail themselves of the primitive accommodation of the rest-house. I believe, however, that except in remote villages where some few recluses maintain the simplicity and austerity of the original orders, a considerable relaxation of the strict rule is not unusual, and the *Pongyi*, at any rate, is not entirely a stranger to greater delicacies than are collected in the mendicant's bowl."
Plates 1 and 2 from a private collection.

Good morning, Spencer. Fondest love. Elgar.

Rangoon. River Scene.

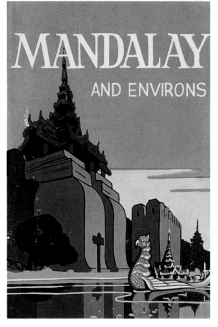

MANDALAY
AND ENVIRONS

THE IRRAWADDY FLOTILLA CO L^D
RANGOON

DOCKYARDS AT RANGOON MANDALAY AND MOULMEIN

to the court at Ava in 1855 to persuade the king to sign a treaty at the conclusion of the Second Anglo-Burmese War, included both an artist and a photographer, as well as officers who surreptitiously and assiduously observed and recorded statistics and facts, collecting information on every subject from language, folklore and architectural history to the presence of coal-bearing strata along the Irrawaddy.

With the incorporation of Burma into Great Britain's Indian Empire, Upper Burma saw an influx of Europeans. While the original campaign had been accomplished relatively swiftly, the pacification of the country as a whole was to take several more years and demanded a growing population of soldiers and civil administrators. Industry and commerce moved in to exploit Burma's natural wealth in oil, teak, rubies and rice. Trade, mail services and passenger travel were carried along the network of river routes maintained by the vessels of the Irrawaddy Flotilla Company, whose sleek paddle-steamers churned the mud of the Irrawaddy from Rangoon to Bhamo on the Chinese border. Founded in the early 1860s, the company had 40 steamers at the time of annexation, but such was the importance of its role in the commercial and administrative infrastructure of the country that, by the 1930s, it was running the largest river fleet in the world, with 270 steamers, as well as a greater number of flats and barges.

For the visitor to Burma with time in hand, the Flotilla's vessels were the obvious means of travel. Writing in *Wanderings in Burma* (1897), the most substantial early guidebook to the country, G W Bird noted that these handsome Clyde-built vessels, "of the most approved and modern type", offered the ideal means of travel, giving the voyager the benefit of viewing the unfolding panorama of Burmese life (both on the deck and on shore) from a vantage point of comfort in which "splendid saloon accommodation is provided, and the fixtures and fittings are most superb…. It is not a matter of surprise, therefore, that a trip from or to Mandalay is so appreciated by all who have the good fortune to seek a change in travel".

The 1890s proved to be a heyday for tourists to Burma. It spawned a host of travel books describing the attractions of a country now securely under British administration, but still providing a frisson of the excitement of the old days of oriental despotism. For these adventurous visitors, Rangoon was usually little more than a starting point, dismissed by many as a prosperous but uninteresting colonial capital. Indeed, Gwendoline Trench Gascoigne, who decided to visit Burma while making "the usual respectable, stereotype Indian tour" in the mid-1890s, at first found almost everything "ugly and unattractive", while

1. Burmese paddy boats on the Irrawaddy, 1890s. The distinctive local craft was the paddy boat or *laung-zat*. These boats, immediately recognizable by their curious bipod masts supporting a long flexible yard on which an enormous spread of sail was carried, were used to transport the rice harvest down the Irrawaddy. The high stern quarters on which the helmsman sat were generally elaborately and intricately carved.
2. 1890s' postcard view of the Rangoon landing stage shows the steamer 'Manwyne' at her berth.

Built on the Clyde in 1887, she was one of the minority of the flotilla's fleet that sailed out to Burma rather than being assembled in the Rangoon company dockyard.
3 and 4. Tourism advertisement and illustration.
5. The Strand Hotel, Rangoon, *circa* 1900. Opened in 1899, the Strand was part of the empire of the Armenian Sarkies brothers, who in the last quarter of the 19th century established a chain of luxury hotels to capture the growing tourist market in Southeast Asia.
6. The Great Bell at Mingun, late 1880s, the largest bell in Burma and reputedly the second largest in the world. Mingun, situated on the right bank of the river a few miles north of Mandalay, was a popular tourist destination.
All Plates from a private collection.

the smoking chimneys of the rice mills reminded her "very unpleasantly of Birmingham, Sheffield, or Leeds". But she too was soon entranced both by the people and the beauty of the Shwedagon pagoda and set off for Mandalay, albeit by train, seduced by the country. But for most visitors, like Mrs Ernest Hart, author of *Picturesque Burma Past and Present* (1897), the river route was the only true approach to Upper Burma, a journey of tropical ease, as for the ten days of the steamer's journey "the idle day passed idly along", punctuated by the calls of the soundsman, the sights of Burmese village life and an unfolding pageant of natural beauty interspersed with crumbling pagodas and the ruined cities of ancient dynasties: Pagan, Ava, Amarapura and finally Mandalay. And at dinner, as the tropical night swiftly fell, "the small party of travellers gathers round the dinner-table in the bows, and until a late hour the captain entertains them with yarns about the stirring times of the recent past: tales of dacoity, and King Thibaw and his ruthless queen, of deeds of blood, violence, and heroism enacted in these very riverside villages".

But if the traveller on the Irrawaddy passed the overgrown ruins of former capitals, the romance of Mandalay itself was of a more modern sort, as it had only been chosen as the new capital by King Mindon in 1857. The belief that human sacrifices were buried at each corner of the new city may only have been a product of the over-heated western imagination, but of the select band of Europeans who had visited Mandalay during its period as the capital of the Kingdom of Ava, the city still presented a series of violent contrasts and excitement: Sir George Scott (of "Scott of the Shan Hills" fame) in the early 1880s found "jewel-studded temples and gilded monasteries standing side by side with wattled hovels...the busy Chinaman next door to the gambling scum of the low country...and over all hanging the fear of prison with its nameless horrors, and the knife of the assassin...". For such old Burma hands British rule in Upper Burma signified an inevitable dilution of the romance of old Mandalay and many indulged in unashamed nostalgia for more uncertain times when there was still a whiff of danger in the air. For Scott, Mandalay under British rule was "vastly less interesting than it used to be...." while "A, B and C roads testify to the unromantic stolidity of the Military Intelligence department". Worse still, the "agreeable scallywags" had now been replaced by "Cook's tourists", while the Palace, "instead of being tawdrily magnificent, smells horribly of bats".

For Mrs Hart, however, enough remained of the past to summon up the ghosts of earlier days. She particularly enjoyed the sight of the palace at dusk when, seen against the sunset, its "barbaric magnificence" was at its most impressive and induced a brooding and melancholy sense of human transience. "Now their glory is departed; the gold leaf is peeling off and is not being replaced, the looking-glass mosaics are grey with dust, the lofty halls have been rifled of their costly decorations, Queen Supayah Lat's audience chamber is the headquarters of the English Club...".

And the city continued to exert its enchantments: by the 1920s it had become a standard point on the eastern tourist's itinerary, as the intrepid ladies of the 1890s were succeeded by other travellers. While the years of British military occupation had inevitably left a legacy of whitewash and corrugated iron in parts of the palace precincts, enough of the magic survived for the sensitive visitor to recreate, at least briefly, something of the gaudy magnificence of Thibaw's capital. One of the more eccentric visitors to city, Major R Raven-Hart even voiced his heretical regret in *Canoe to Mandalay* (1939) that the Burmese monarchy had not been retained, "so that the Palace would be a living thing today instead of an empty shell, and Burmese art and music and literature would flourish in its shadow".

Mandalay was once more to be the centre of historic events, when in March 1945 it was the scene of bitter fighting as General Slim's army recaptured the town from the Japanese. In the course of the struggle King Thibaw's palace was burnt to the ground, but in the evening light the restored buildings still summon up an echo of its former glory. For throughout all the vicissitudes of its history, Burma has managed to retain the power to impress its spell on even the most fleeting visitor. This Kipling realized from his first glimpse of the Shwedagon pagoda against the skyline: "Then, a golden mystery upheaved itself on the horizon...a shape that was neither Muslim dome nor Hindu temple spire...the golden dome said: 'This is Burma, and it will be quite unlike any land you know about!'"

1 and 2. Late 19th-century photographs of Burmese women. The independence and openness of Burmese women compared to Indian and other Asian races were traits remarked on by almost all European visitors. Major-General A Ruxton MacMahon notes in *Far Cathay and Farther India* (1893): "Even a casual traveller like [Lady Violet Greville writing in *Nineteenth Century*] notices that the independence of Burmese women is remarkable. They manage their own affairs, hold stalls in the bazaar with which no one interferes, marry when they choose, and divorce their husbands as soon as they please. No jealous veils cover their faces, no melancholy purdah seclusion prevents them from mixing with the male sex. They flirt, dance, and laugh with as many admirers as they choose, and, last of all, they smoke–not dainty little cigarettes...but cigars! cigars longer than men use in Europe; cigars a foot long.... [truly] Burma is the land of women par excellence'"

3. Painting in the Shwe-In-bin monastery, Mandalay, by Hsaya Saw, 2nd half of 19th century. It depicts a colonial pulled up short by the beauty of Burma's girls.

4. The hairy family of Mandalay, 1880s. The human curiosity of the Burmese hairy family had fascinated Europeans for many years and several of the early missions to Burma had encountered examples. John Crawfurd had met Shwe-maong in the 1820s and his daughter Maphoon was similarly presented to members of the British Mission to Ava in 1855, who described the hair covering her face as like "the wisps of a fine Skye terrier's coat". Despite her appearance, "Poor Maphoon's manners were good and modest, her voice soft and feminine, and her expression mild and not unpleasing". Plates 1, 2 and 4 from a private collection.

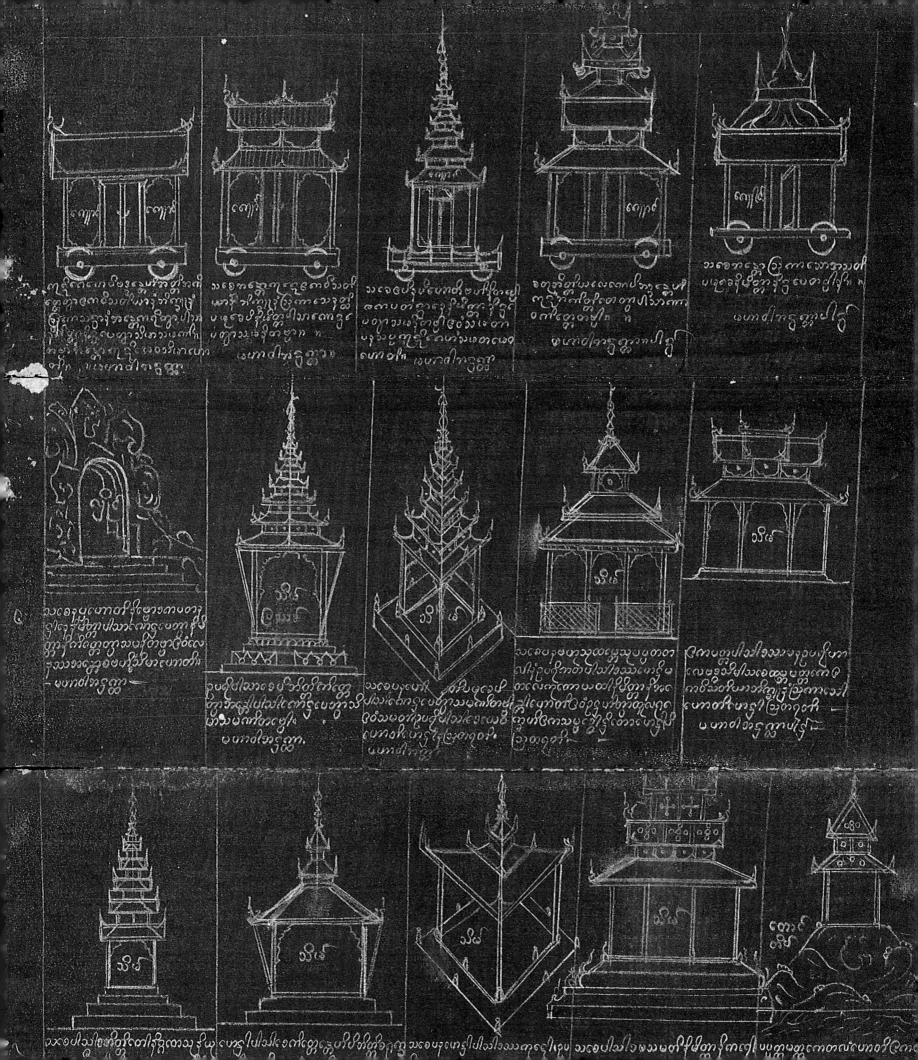

Religious Architecture

The richness of religious architecture in Myanmar reflects the continuity of Buddhist tradition over at least the last 2,000 years. It embraces a range of structures, from wooden monasteries to gilded pagodas. Similarly, the everyday religious life of Buddhist Myanmar incorporates a great array of offerings, festivals, and other acts of devotion. The importance of religious donation has long encouraged innovation, and contemporary architectural embellishments include brightly coloured paint, constant white-washing to renew a temple, glittering mirrors and neon lights.

However, throughout the country, the forms remain much the same as in the past. The most frequently seen is the stupa or *zeidi* (the "golden pagodas" of Myanmar). There are many types, all based on the same combination of elements. The *anda* or bell—likened to the *thabeik* or begging bowl carried by Buddhist monks—of the pagoda rests on square and octagonal terraces. Above the bell are a series of shapes: rings, petals of the lotus flower, the *hnget-pyaw-bu* or banana bud. Some people say the form of the banana bud comes from the shape made by two hands held in prayer although there is no proof for this. Above the banana bud is the umbrella or *hti*, and the flag-like vane. At the summit of the pagoda is the orb, symbol of Nirvana, ultimate enlightenment and release from rebirth.

The stupa evolved from burial mounds in India, before the time of the 6th-century BC Buddha Gotama. After his enlightenment, his relics were distributed and enshrined within stupas. Stupas in India are solid structures, but in Myanmar there are some that may be entered. Temples in Myanmar were more common at the 9th–13th-century royal city of Bagan (Pagan) than in subsequent eras. These temples range from small single-celled shrines to massive two-storey edifices. Most temples have one principal entry with false doors on the other façades, although others may be entered on all four sides. Whatever the size and plan of the temple, it sheltered an image. In nearly all cases, this was an image of the Buddha, although typically in Myanmar, there are exceptions to the rule!

Previous Page. The 12th-century Ananda temple, now considered the apogee of Bagan's architectural heritage.
1. Details drawn using a white steatite crayon on a "black" *parabaik* or folding manuscript illustrate the importance of roofs in Burmese religious architecture, including the many variations of the multiple-storied *pyat-that*. Black *parabaik* were folded accordion-style with the long strips of handmade paper made from the bark of the mulberry tree. The paper was then coated with a mixture of powdered charcoal, rice water and animal hide glue. The coating process allowed the *parabaik* to be re-used several times. Courtesy of Beikthano Gallery, Yangon.
2. Old photographs from the 1880s record the ornate carving of the Mandalay palace. *Pyat-that* tiered roofs graced the many throne rooms, and also, as here, over the main image of the Queen's monastery. The *pyat-that* is seen today in the recently reconstructed Mandalay palace, and over countless images of the Buddha in the monasteries of Myanmar. This use in both royal and religious contexts typifies the close links between kingship and Buddhism in forming Myanmar's cultural heritage. Photograph from a private collection.

1

1. The ancient city of Bagan
stretches out along the bank of the
Irrawaddy River. Although rich and
green during the summer monsoon
months, the rains reaching the
Bagan plain are sparse compared
to the delta region of Yangon
During the rest of the year, Bagan
receives virtually no rain. Scholars
once wondered if the environment
was lush during the city's 9th–13th-
century heyday, but it is now
agreed that today's arid ecology
was also present in the past.

Stupas and temples are found within the same enclosure at ancient and modern Buddhist sites in Myanmar.
Today, many stupas sit at the centre of a rectangular or
square compound made up of many smaller shrines,
each within its own building. Some may house images
other than the Buddha, for example, the territorial spirit
of the pagoda, the Bo Bo Gyi. There are also planetary
posts associated with different days of the week. A
visit to the pagoda may include not only veneration of
the central stupa but offerings made within a number
of shrines and at one of the planetary posts. We cannot be certain, but this array of ritual locales probably
characterized ancient pagoda compounds as well.

Continuous traditions are also found in Burmese
monastery architecture. Certain forms within the area
of the monastery mirror those of the pagoda compound. Both monastery and temple may be crowned
by a tiered roof, the *pyat-that*. Images or relics of the
Buddha occupy the spiritual heart of monastery and
pagoda enclosures, and monasteries may have an

associated stupa or temple. An outer wall attached to
the temple, within which the monks undoubtedly lived,
surrounds many of the temples and stupas of Bagan.
Evidence for this is seen in recesses on the sides of
brick temples meant to support wooden structures.
Reconstructions show these would have been similar
to more recent wooden monasteries.

Some of the earliest religious buildings are found at
sites of the Pyu peoples, a race later absorbed by
the Tibeto-Burmans. Brick structures at Thayekhittaya
(Srikshetra, Prome or Pyay) are dated to the 5th–8th
century. At the 9th–13th-century city of Bagan, the
religious remains number in the thousands. Further
north is the last royal capital, Mandalay. The city was
founded in the 19th century, although pagodas such
as the Bagan-period Shwekyimyint testify to earlier
settlement. The country's most sacred image of the
Buddha rests within the Mahamuni (Hpayagyi) pagoda
in Mandalay. Clustered around Mandalay, on the same
bank of the great Irrawaddy River, are many earlier

sites. There is Ava (Inwa), capital in the 13th and 17th centuries. Between Ava and Mandalay is Amarapura, the seat of the Konbaung Dynasty in the late 18th and early 19th century. On the opposite bank of the Irrawaddy is Sagaing, long renowned as a centre of retreat and religious meditation. King Bowdawpaya, who reigned from 1782–1819, built many temples at Sagaing, and further north, at Mingun. The most revered pagoda of all, the Shwedagon, lies far to the south at the heart of the present capital, Yangon. According to traditional history, the Shwedagon was founded during the lifetime of the Buddha and enshrines eight sacred hairs brought back from India by two merchant brothers.

The earliest remaining brick buildings are found at Pyu sites dating from the 1st–11th centuries. Some of these, such as the complex of monastic cells at the ancient Pyu city of Beikthano (a Burmese corruption of "Vishnu City") dated 1st–5th century, southeast of Bagan, clearly derive from Indian prototypes. In the case of the Beikthano monastery, the complex is likened to those at Nagarajunakonda in South India. The script on a terracotta seal from the site has been used to date it to the 2nd century.

Other Pyu buildings present more difficult attributions in their form and use. For example, at Halin (9–11th century, north of Mandalay), there are unusual remains of square brick structures with a central stupa. Both inhumation burials and cremation urns have been re-covered around the shrines. The heads of two recently excavated skeletons pointed to the southeast, with urns grouped around their heads. The southeast is generally the direction of the house spirit or *ein-saung nat*, and south the location of village spirit shrines.

Neither of these architectural forms is seen in later periods, illustrating the gaps in our knowledge of early Indic influences in Burmese religious architecture. The stupa, however, not only continued, but dominated religious construction after Bagan. Thayekhittaya has

three bulbous stupas dating to about the 9th century. All three are outside the 12-km long circular brick wall that surrounds the ancient city. Their position, and later alterations, makes a firm dating impossible. However, their presence is used to place the few bulbous stupas at Bagan early in the city's history.

One of the Bagan bulbous stupas is aptly called Nga-kwe-na-daung, or "ear ornament of Nga-kywe", in reference to the plug-like earrings of the Bagan period. Traces of green glazing remain on the Nga-kwe-na-daung, evidence of a ceramic expertise that has yet to be fully documented. Another bulbous stupa, the Bupaya, has received donations over the centuries, for it also houses the guardian spirit of the Irrawaddy River on whose bank it stands. It was greatly damaged in the earthquake of 1975, but today is smooth and gilded, pristine and beautiful, but an archaeological enigma. The dating of both bulbous stupas is uncertain but they are commonly placed in the 9th–10th century, as the city wall of Bagan is traditionally dated to the mid-9th century.

Brick temples or *gu* are found at pre-Bagan Pyu sites, most notably Thayekhittaya. As with the bulbous stupas it is their location rather than any epigraphic evidence that has given rise to a pre-Bagan dating. In fact, they are little different in form from many of the single-celled brick temples attributed to later periods. Eclecticism and variation mark all of Myanmar's religious architecture. The variation in temple form encouraged an equally broad repertoire of interior donations. Mural paintings once covered the walls and ceilings of Bagan's temples; some of these remain today, making them the earliest surviving wall paintings in the region.

Myanmar has a long and rich woodcarving tradition. The wooden shrines which house many of the animistic spirit or *nat* figures suggest that forms of religious architecture preceded the adoption of Indic norms. Given the tropical climate, we have little remaining evidence of wooden structures. Even at Bagan, where thousands of brick temples survive, we know little of the wooden palaces and houses that would have made up the ancient city.

Bagan does, however, provide evidence of contemporary wooden architecture in its mural paintings and temple architecture. For example, at the 11th-century Nanpaya and other early temples, a *pyat-that* surmounts the windows. At later temples, monasteries and palaces, the *pyat-that* recurs again and again. The number of tiers of a *pyat-that* varies, but is always uneven. In monastic compounds (*kyaung*) the *pyat-that* crowns the room housing the main image, while in palace architecture it crowned not only images of

the Buddha but throne rooms of the king. It is recognized as the hallmark of monastery architecture, and is seen in countless examples from the massive Bagaya *kyaung* at Ava to the many monasteries (excluding the Atumashi) of Mandalay.

Myanmar's religious shrines are part of the landscape. All are dedicated to the *hpaya* or Lord Buddha, their verticality replicating the towering Mount Meru at the centre of the Buddhist cosmos. The religious architecture creates the spaces for sacred relics and to accommodate ritual. All evoke man's earthly hopes and his relationship to the divine. Whether the rounded form of a stupa or the tiered roof of a *pyat-that*, each marks a venerated place in the terrain. When the locales, structures, images, relics and offerings are multiplied to include all the country, one begins to understand the power and significance of religious architecture in historic and present-day Myanmar.

1	2

1. The image of the Buddha glows in the dimly lit interior of the Shwenandaw monastery in Mandalay. It sits upon an elaborately carved throne, gilded and adorned with mirrors. The massive teak columns and carved surround are also gilded, aptly recalling its name "royal golden" monastery. A *saing-baung*, the form of a wild-ox's haunch, curves on both sides at the top of the surround. The roundels flanking the Buddha contain carvings of a peacock and rabbit, symbols of the sun and moon.

2. Many of Myanmar's splendid wooden monasteries have sadly fallen victim to fire and war. One casualty has been the beautifully carved Queen's monastery. (The *pyat-that* over the main image of the Buddha is seen on page 21.) The queen ordered its construction inside the palace grounds in 1885. In addition to the wood-carving, detailed glass mosaics set in the wood panels added to the rich decoration. Private collection.

Bagan

agan (Pagan) is unique in many respects. The ancient royal city was and is renowned as a centre of Buddhism. It is located along the bank of the Irrawaddy River in an extremely arid region of the country. Undoubtedly the dry climate attracted ancient settlement of the site. It has also assisted in its preservation, notably of mural paintings on the interior of a great number of its temples. More than 13,000 stupas and temples may be dated to its zenith, the 11th to 13th century. Today more than 5,000 of these structures remain, presenting an extraordinary variety of form and ornamentation.

Bagan is not a concentrated urban area, although part of it is enclosed within a city wall dated to the mid-9th century. The temples are not, however, restricted to the walled enclosure, but spread over some 30 square km along the east bank of the river. The legendary founding of the city dates it to the early 2nd century, but its history and temples become better documented from the reign of King Anawratha (r. 1044–77). The role of Bagan diminished after the 1283 Mongol invasion from the north; nonetheless, royal and religious donations continued. There are, for example, mural paintings in temple libraries dated to the 17th century, and simple wooden monasteries dated to the 20th century.

The earliest religious structures at Bagan are stupas, but there are more temples than stupas amongst the multitude of buildings. The first temples are lower, usually only single storied, whereas the later temples include huge edifices of two stories or a series of

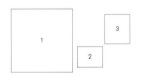

1. The Bupaya stands proudly on the shores of the Irrawaddy River. Its fresh painted and gilded superstructure are the result of repairs following damage to the stupa in the 1075 earthquake. The Bupaya is dated to the 9th century based on similarities to Pyu stupas. It is located at one end of the city wall that is also traditionally dated to the same period.
2. The early 12th-century Ananda continues today as a centre of worship. Pilgrims flock to this temple for the annual pagoda festival held on the Full Moon Day of January. The four arms of the temple point in towards the central core. Glazed plaques adorn the exterior at both ground level and along the upper terraces. As there is no access to the upper levels, it seems the primary motivation of the builder, King Kyanzittha, was to accumulate merit rather than to spread the wisdom of the Buddha.
3. The 11th-century Shwesandaw is one of the four massive stupas built by King Anawratha to mark the limits of his city. The tall terraces and proportions of the *anda* (bell) differ greatly from the Shwezigon, another of Anawratha's stupas. The absence of norms for contemporary structures make it difficult to establish a stylistic progression amongst Bagan's stupas.

pyramidal tiers surmounting the base. The temples are rich in Buddhist, and to a lesser extent, Brahmanic images. These include relief carvings, paintings, and the image at the heart of the shrine. Many of these principal images of the Buddha are brick, coated in stucco and painted. Others were finely carved from sandstone, sometimes covered in lacquer and gilt. A few are hollow lacquer, delicately created over a core. Later images may be concrete, gilded, or painted.

The principal image of most temples is that of the last Buddha, the 6th-century BC Gotama. However, at the Ananda temple the central pillar is flanked by the last four Buddhas of our era. The Buddha or Buddhas, are the reliquary core of the temple, just as the stupa marks the location of precious relics. The main image is seated on a throne at the heart of the temple, both literally and spiritually.

1. Guardian or *dvarapala* figures flank the tall arched doorway of the 11th–early 12th-century Nagayon temple. Their graceful curves are formed from stucco applied over brick. Traces of mural paintings remain on the walls behind.
2. The form of the Nagayon temple typifies much of the so-called early architecture of Bagan. Several broad terraces lead the eye up to the rounded *sikhara* that surmounts its base.
3. One of three images of the Buddha in the Nagayon's inner shrine. The tall standing image displays the *abhaya mudra*, the Buddha dispelling fear.
4. The stone of the 11th-century, sandstone Nanpaya temple has been cut to form brick-like shapes. These have weathered to a soft golden brown hue. The perforated windows are surmounted by the tiers of a *pyat-that* executed in stone. Above, a row of *hintha* or *hamsa* birds make a further decorative band. Each *hintha* sits within a roundel or *tondo*.
5. An empty plinth sits at the centre of the inner shrine of the Nanpaya. Four massive pillars mark the corners of the plinth. The inner face of each pillar is carved with a graceful figure generally identified as Brahma with his four faces. Some identify the figures as *bodhisattvas* or Buddhas-to-be. As the central plinth is thought to have held an image of the Buddha, guardian *bodhisattvas* rather than Brahmanic deities would give the temple a totally Buddhist attribution. Both identifications must be considered, especially as Brahmanic and Buddhist iconography was often used within the same temple.

Most of Bagan's stupas and temples are constructed of brick. There are a few notable exceptions, such as the sandstone Nanpaya. Bricks were donated by the surrounding villages, and some were stamped with a village name. When a building was completed, it was coated both inside and out, using a combination of glazing, stuccowork and painting. Some pagodas have traces of a green ceramic glaze, including the 9th–10th century bulbous stupa, the Nga-kywe-na-daung. Terracotta plaques were often used to adorn stupa exteriors, while temples were coated with stucco on the outside and decorated with mural paintings within.

The stucco was beautifully applied to the brick surfaces. Swirling floral curves contrast with the strong and straight horizontal lines of tiered roofs or *pyat-that* over many of the windows along the sides of the temples. The origins of Bagan's stuccowork are uncertain, and

even though stucco from the 6th–9th century remains at Nakhon Pathom in the central zone of neighbouring Thailand, pre-Bagan stucco has yet to be found in Myanmar. Stucco reliefs of the *Jatakas* (life stories of the Buddha) are fluidly executed, with lively, lithe figures.

The same skill may have formed part of the Mon contribution to Bagan. When King Anawratha captured the southern Mon port of Thaton in the 11th century, he brought Mon artisans to Bagan. The 10th–early 12th-century one-storey temples of Bagan are often called "early" and labelled "Mon". Many have Mon inscriptions, but the term is also used to describe a love of dark and mysterious interiors. This is an aesthetic and qualitative judgement for which evidence is lacking.

The one-storey temples have a very different atmosphere from the later two-storey structures. However, we cannot be sure this is a reflection of Mon taste at the time. Mons, Pyus, and Burmans all contributed to the architecture, sculpture and mural paintings which

illustrate admirably the cosmopolitan life of the ancient city. Particularly apparent are interaction with Bengal in Northeast India, Tibet to the north of Myanmar, and traders arriving along the Silk Route. In addition to overland trade, changes also came via the massive Irrawaddy River. The religious architecture of Bagan beautifully displays all these influences.

Even though some forms—such as the bulbous stupa—disappear in later Bagan architecture and towering two-storey temples appear only in the last phases of the city's history, a clear architectural evolution cannot be defined. Generalizations diminish its stupendous architectural breadth. The sheer range of forms and motifs may be the result of patronage with each donor perhaps wishing to outdo his or her predecessor in order to accumulate ever-greater merit, or they may be a result of religious preferences. Not only are the plans of each temple different, but there is an equal degree of innovation in the content of the mural paintings within many of the interiors.

| 1 | | 3 |
| 2 | | 4 |

1. The enormous Dhammayangyi temple lies east of Bagan's city wall. Dated to the second half of the 12th century, it was never completed. Like the Ananda, the plan is that of a Greek cross with four arms projecting from the central core.
2. The Buddhas within the interior niches depart radically from earlier images. Here the large rounded head of the Buddha sits firmly on rounded shoulders. Earlier images had V-shaped faces, pointed chins, slender necks, broader shoulders.
3. The 12th-century Thatbyinnyu temple rises high above the dry plain of Bagan. The main image is sheltered in the tall upper storey, its square form clearly separated from the lower terraces.
4. Countless images of the Buddha are found within the temple. The posture of the bronze image here mirrors the sweeping curve of the arch that shelters it.

Jatakas varies. At some temples the squares are five cm on each side, at others as much as a foot. In still other temples, only the last ten *Jatakas* are shown, in long continuous narrative strips. In eras before our own, Buddhas also existed and Myanmar Buddhism counts 28 previous Buddhas. At Bagan these are often shown in a row at the top of a wall covered with mural paintings accompanied by an explanatory legend. The rich interior decoration is completed by the floral and vegetal motifs. These fill the wall spaces, the deep-set arches over windows, and the ceiling. The overall effect is sumptuous as if the temple is swathed in textiles and carpets.

Exterior decoration is equally diverse, but much has been lost over the centuries. When Bagan was a living city, a complex urban area, a royal capital as well as a centre of religious education, it was a clear demonstration of pious donation and merit making. Today, however, only the mass of Bagan's brick structures remain stretching out over the arid plain. Yet from the curves of the stupas, *sikharas* and vaulted arches to the peaks of the umbrellas or *htis* reaching heavenwards, they endure as a testimony to the living tradition of Buddhism in contemporary Myanmar.

Bagan is alone among the ancient capitals of Southeast Asia in the preservation of mural painting from this period (*see pages 154–161*). The paintings were applied to dry plaster walls in colours that came from natural sources such as charcoal, ochres and lime. Other materials—many of which were vegetal and animal substances—were mixed with the pigments to help them adhere to the wall.

There is extraordinary variety in the mural paintings. Scenes from the life of the Buddha often surround the temple's main image, with eight events usually shown. These are: the Buddha's birth; his enlightenment; the first sermon; the twin miracles; the descent from Tavatimsa heaven; the Parileyyaka retreat when the Buddha is honoured by an elephant and a monkey; the taming of the Nalagiri elephant; the Buddha's death and ascent or Parinirvana.

The 550 previous lives of the Buddha are also depicted. Each is framed in a square with a schematic representation of the story elements. The size of the rows of

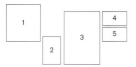

1. The Mahabodhi temple takes its form from the famous structure at Bodhgaya. Its truncated *sikhara* provides a contrast to the more usual rounded *sikhara* of Bagan. Architects from Bagan travelled to Bodhgaya in previous centuries to carry out repairs. Here the early 13th-century structure faithfully follows the original.
2. The late 11th–early 12th century Gawdawpalin on the banks of the Irrawaddy is a favourite spot from which to watch the sun sink behind the hills on the opposite bank of the river. Its superstructure was badly damaged in the 1975 earthquake, but extensive repairs have preserved the towering landmark.
3. The Htilominlo lies north of the city wall, its bulk unmistakable along the road to the town of Nyaung U. Dated to

the early 13th century, this temple takes its form from the earlier Sulamani temple. The broad but sharp terraces mark the transition from the base to the upper block.
4. The late 13th-century Thambula temple lacks the large upper storey that typifies the end of the Bagan period. Antechambers mark the four sides providing entry to the central cell. Despite the absence of a block-like super-structure, a staircase allows ascent to the higher levels.
5. The late 13th-century Hpaya-thonzu (literally the three caves dedicated to the *hpaya* or lord) forms part of the Minnanthu group. The exquisite paintings in the interior depict curvaceous *bodhisattvas* and their *sakti* or consorts. These and other elements of the iconography link the group to Tantric or Mahayanist practices. Overleaf. Buddhas rest peacefully within the late 12th-century Sulamani temple. The bright exterior sunlight filters softly into the ambulatory corridor. Traces of post-Bagan paintings remain on the walls.

Mrauk-U (Rakhine)

The Rakhine (Arakan) State of northwest Myanmar had a long and rich history as an independent state until the 18th century when it was invaded by the Myanmar king, Bodawpaya. As part of his conquest, Bodawpaya removed the venerated Hpayagyi image of the Buddha. Traditional histories record a visit of the 6th-century BC Buddha Gotama to Arakan. The early history of the region continues with ancient sites such as Vesali (Wethali) dated to the 2nd century BC. The most splendid of the old cities is the 15th–18th-century Buddhist site of Mrauk-U where stupa upon stupa rest among rugged hills bounding the remains.

Although it is situated some 45 miles inland from the coast of the Bay of Bengal, Rakhine's strategic loca-

tion between India and the islands to the east brought prosperity. It also brought European visitors who spoke glowingly of its riches. A Dutchman in the 16th century compared Mrauk-U to Amsterdam and London!

The architecture of Rakhine is unique and very different from the rest of Myanmar. Especially in the monuments dating from the 15th and 16th centuries, the affinity with the tradition of Bihar is more evident than any influence from Upper Burma. The two main characteristics are the combined use of brick and stone and the fortress-like appearance of the religious buildings, enclosed by massive walls almost devoid of any decoration. Often built atop a hill, these were used as refuges during the frequent wars. The many narrow passages and corridors, however, were embellished by a multitude of decorations and carvings, often rendered in a naive style.

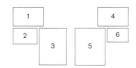

1. The Ley Myet Nha or "four faces or façades" pagoda was built in 1430 by the first king of Mrauk-U. The central cell is octagonal but surmounted by a domed stupa. Four passageways protrude from the sides of the cell. Inside, each side of the inner chamber has 28 niches sheltering images of the previous Buddhas.
2. Paper-fine gold leaves cover the shrine of a spirit figure during an annual festival.
3. Many finely carved figures are found in the inner gallery of the Shitthaung temple. The gallery is vaulted and decorated with several tiers in high relief. There are mainly Buddhist, but also Brahmanic images, mythical creatures such as the *kinnari*, and amorous figures.
4. The 1571 Dukkanthein (Htukkanthein) pagoda is built principally of sandstone, with a brick superstructure, as are the Andaw and Shitthaung

temples. As at the Shitthaung, fine carvings adorn the inner corridor. Many female figures, seated and offering lotus buds, are said to have been the wives of noblemen displaying 64 different hairstyles.
5. The Andaw Shrine (1521) contains a tooth relic of the Buddha said to have been acquired by the king from Sri Lanka. The main stupa is octagonal, constructed of sandstone, although the 15 smaller shrines that surround it (seen here) are brick.
6. The Shitthaung temple or "shrine of 80,000 images", is dated to 1535. Lying north of the city's palace site, its formidable mass has been called more of a fortress than a pagoda. Like many of Rakhine's temples, the broad base and carvings of the Shitthaung are made of sandstone. A ten-foot tall stone pillar on the north entry of the Shitthaung is inscribed in Sanskrit dated paleographically to the 6th–8th century. The pillar is said to have been brought to Mrauk-U from the ancient city of Vesali.
All Plates photographed by Jean-Léo Dugast. Photobank.

Ava

Ava (Inwa) had two periods of greatness, first as a Shan kingdom in the 14th–16th century, and then as the centre of Burmese power from the 17th century to the founding of Amarapura in the late 18th century. The site is filled with ancient remains now beginning to be excavated and restored: These include the masonry watch tower of the 19th-century King Bagyidaw and the distinctive Inwa-style of *pyat-that* on the city walls. Also of interest is the brick and stucco Maha Aungmye Bonzan monastery, built by Bagyidaw's chief queen in 1818. It suffered damage in an earthquake in 1838, but was repaired by the queen of King Mindon. Its ornate brickwork and stucco mirror those of wooden monasteries.

Monasteries and pagodas are scattered around the area within the old city walls. In the southern side of the city can be found the remains of the four-storey Leidatgyi temple, while further south is the Ava Fort. One of the finest monasteries is the early 20th-century wooden Bagaya *kyaung*, built with 267 teak posts. A community of monks still lives there, fulfilling a vital role in teaching lay people and encouraging the support and involvement of the surrounding community. This presence of ancient and modern monasteries in Ava (as elsewhere) reflects the continuing importance of the *Sangha* or monkhood in Myanmar's religious and secular life.

1. Fine, intricate stuccowork on the exterior of the Leidatgyi temple is a characteristic of the religious architecture of the Late Ava period.
2. Remains of stupas, some dating back to the Bagan period, abound within the outer walls of Ava. While some are neglected, neighbouring stupas have profited from pious donations. For example, the shrine in the distance, and its fierce *naga* or serpent guarding the image of the Buddha, are all freshly painted.
3. A large *chinthe* or mythical lion stands guard at the ancient city of Ava.
4. Monks used the main prayer room of the Maha Aungmye Bonzan, the *saung-ma-gyi* for prayer and teaching. At the far end the tiered roof the *pyat-that* marks the main shrine room of the monastery, the *hpaya-saung*.
5. The massive Bagaya *kyaung* is crowned by the multiple tiers of a *pyat-that*.

Amarapura

The religious architecture of Ava, Amarapura, Mingun and Sagaing is less well known than that of Bagan, but forms a rich and distinct heritage spanning the 14th–19th centuries. Located on the west bank of the Irrawaddy River, Amarapura is literally called city (*pura*) of immortality (*amara*).

In 1783 the capital shifted from Ava to Amarapura under King Bodawpaya, but moved back to Ava under his grandson, King Bagyidaw, in 1823. Change came once more with the next reign, that of King Tharawaddy, who again left Ava for Amarapura. The king and his court remained at Amarapura until King Mindon founded the last royal city of Myanmar, Mandalay, in 1856. Each time the king moved, the wooden palace was dismantled and rebuilt in the new locale. Thus, although repairs, renovations and innovations were carried out, the form of royal architecture remained much the same for many centuries.

In contrast, the religious architecture of all four cities is characterized by its variability. The basic elements of the temples and stupas stayed constant, but there was increasing elaboration in decorative aspects. This may have been the result of increased and varied

1. Small stupas mark the corners of the Patodawgyi's lower terraces. *Jatakas*, stories of the former lives of the Buddha, are carved on marble slabs adorning the terraces.
2. A *manuthiha* sits in front of a row of *sein-daung*, a row of upright leaves. *Sein-daung* are seen on a number of structures such as monasteries and rest houses (*zayat*). The motif also adorns palanquins and military helmets. The *manuthiha* has a human head with a double lion body. The creature is associated with the Mon peoples of Myanmar: it was created long ago to frighten an ogre and ogress that had been terrorizing the countryside by eating small children.
3. The large *naga*, or serpent, that gives the Nagayon its name rises up to shelter the shrine containing the main image of the Buddha. The corners of the two upper terraces are marked with small *manuthiha*, while a massive footed dragon, or *naya*, borders the staircase.

1. The early 19th-century Shwegugyi pagoda is seen in the distance, viewed from the upper terraces of the nearby Patodawgyi pagoda.
2. The varied shrines of the Thatta Htarna monastery sit in a wooded area popular for meditation.
3. This small rounded stupa sits well guarded, with *chinthe* or mythical lions at each corner of the platform and rearing *nayas* cascading down the stairs.

patronage. Chinese and European influence can also be seen, adding new motifs and forms to the architectural repertoire.

Amarapura was laid out as a vast square, walled and surrounded by a moat. A central landmark is the unusual, early 19th-century Nagayon pagoda. One of the most well known pagodas is the Patodawgyi, built by King Bagyidaw in 1820, shortly before he shifted the capital back to Ava. It sits just outside the old city wall on the south. Further south is the vast Taungthaman Lake, traversed by a massive wooden bridge, over a km long, built from the posts of the earlier palace at Ava. The Kyauktawgyi pagoda (1847) is at the end of this bridge. It is said to have been modelled on the Ananda at Bagan. Mural paintings adorn its east and west interior, providing not only a valuable record of monastic architecture in the 19th century, but examples of a number of earlier pagodas renovated by the king. A number of smaller shrines are found in the wooded area around the Kyauktawgyi.

Mingun

Mingun is best known for its massive, unfinished pagoda, started by King Bodawpaya while he reigned at Amarapura. He died, in 1819, before it was completed. Although only the lower terrace of the pagoda was built, it is the biggest pile of bricks in the world. If construction had finished, it would have been the largest pagoda in Myanmar, rising a reputed 150 metres. As spectacular as the size of the Mingun pagoda are the large fissures in its walls, the result of the 1838 earthquake. Nearby is another of Bodawpaya's acts of merit, the 87-ton Mingun bell, said to be the second largest bell in the world.

Other pagodas dot the riverbank around Mingun. One of the largest, the Hshinbyume, was built in 1816 by Bodawpaya's successor, Bagyidaw. He erected the pagoda before ascending the throne, in memory of the death of his main princess. The pagoda replicates the Buddhist cosmos, with seven rows of mountains surrounding the central peak of Mount Meru, home of the god Indra in Tavatimsa heaven. The niches of each level contain the five types of mythical animals who guard the mythical Mount Meru.

Today's visitor reaches Mingun on one of the small ferries that ply the Irrawaddy from Mandalay. It is a quiet, sleepy village, a respite from the city's bustle.

1. The undulating arches, on seven terraces, circle the central stupa of the Hshinbyume pagoda. The upper *zeidi* takes its form from that of the Sulamani pagoda located at the summit of Mount Meru.

2. The circular terraces of the Hshinbyume represent the seven ranges of mountains that encircle Mount Meru.

3. The size of the door within the façade of the huge Mingun pagoda gives some indication of its mass. An entry shrine marks each side of the square base. Much of the decoration was never carried out as its founder, King Bodawpaya, died before the pagoda was completed.

Sagaing

Although Sagaing was a royal capital for a short time in the early 14th century, it is mainly known as a centre of meditation. Devotees from all over the country come to Sagaing to meditate, and—now, as in the past—it houses over 500 monasteries.

Some of these monasteries are of masonry, others deep within caves, and still others nestle in the valleys between the low hills. Mural paintings in caves such as the Tilawkaguru date back several centuries. The famous Kaunghmudaw pagoda was built in the 17th century to house a tooth relic of the Buddha. Its rounded Ceylonese form is unusual for Myanmar, although legends state that its shape mirrored that of the breasts of the king's most beloved wife.

The city can be seen along the river's edge, but quiet and tranquillity are easily found in the endless pagodas of its surrounding hills. Some sit high above the landscape, such as the Soon U Ponya Shin pagoda. From here at sunset, the broad Irrawaddy becomes a dusky violet, its smooth surface reflecting the pagodas along its banks. The outline of Mandalay Hill is sometimes visible, and the blue of the Shan Hills in the distance.

1		
2	3	4

1. The great Irrawaddy flows past Sagaing, with Mandalay on the opposite bank. Pagodas and monasteries are found on top of its countless hills and in its many valleys.
2. A golden reliquary stupa sits within the Soon U Ponya Shin pagoda. The pagoda is said to encase two relics of the Buddha.

3. Caves throughout the Sagaing hills shelter images of the Buddha. The Onhmin Thonze pagoda consists of 30 caves (*thonze*), with a myriad of Buddhas set within its crescent-shaped interior.
4. The square cube of the Soon U Ponya Shin pagoda rises high above the surrounding landscape. Rows of smaller stupas, painted white, mark the pagoda enclosure. The stupa and its *hti* are more than 35 metres high, and give visitors an unrivalled panorama of the surrounding area.

Mandalay

Mandalay Hill was a sacred site long before 1857 when King Mindon began to build his new capital around it. In order to consecrate the new city, seven features (including several religious buildings) needed to be built. These were: the city wall and gates; the moats; the Maha-lawka Marazein (Kuthodaw pagoda); the library (Pitaka-taik); the royal monastery (Kyaung-daw); the Ordination Hall (Dhamma-Myitzu-Thein); and the rest houses (Thu-da-ma Zayat-daw), or else a royal preaching hall (Dhammasala).

The city takes its name from the hill or *taung* around which it is built. Some say the name "Mandalay" came from the Pali word *mandala*, interpreted by Myanmar scholars as an abode of pleasantness where one might seek a religious education. Other stories involve spirits or *nats*. The word "*mingalay*", for example, means "small king". When used at the end of a name, however, it indicates that the person became a *nat*. An exiled son of a Bagan King, Shin Saw Mingalay, is said to have lived on Mandalay Hill, then known as Mingalay Taung. Also, a Pyu princess named Mingalay is said to have visited the hill. The repeated references to royal visitors and to *nats* suggest a long and continuous occupation of the sacred hill.

The royal palace, one of the first buildings to be constructed, lies north of Mandalay Hill. King Mindon used many parts of the teak building from the old capital of Amarapura; these had already been moved from Ava, to Amarapura and back again, to form the royal buildings at Amarapura in 1837. Although the main parts of the palace were used time and time again, each shift added new and ornate carvings, which were painted and then gilded. Also near Mandalay Hill—at its base—are a number of monasteries and pagodas. Enormous *chinthe* (lions) flank the ascent and, at the summit, a large image of the Buddha stands tall. His posture is unusual: the right arm is raised and the index finger points out towards the new city of King Mindon below.

Royal associations and unusual forms typify much of the religious architecture of the city. A number of monasteries are located east of the palace in the old royal quarter. Among these is the Shwenandaw, a beautifully carved teak structure that was originally inside Mandalay palace. A myriad of figures adorns its softly weathered exterior. Inside the main prayer room are elaborately carved and gilded panels of the last ten *Jataka* tales. The buildings formed the private apartments occupied by King Mindon shortly before his death. His successor, King Thibaw, dismantled the apartment in 1880, and moved it east to construct the new monastery.

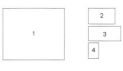

1. The tiers of a *pyat-that* rise behind the *chinthe* guarding the ascent to Mandalay Hill. The *pyat-that* may mark both royal and religious structures. The word "*pyat-that*" comes from the Sanskrit "*prasada*"; a palatial building commonly adorned with multiple roofs. As with the *pyat-that*, the *prasada* was supported by pillars, size being equated with their number.
2. A *bilu* (ogre) outside the Atumashi monastery, prior to recent reconstruction.
3. An old postcard of the Atumashi showing the ornate stuccowork that adorned the wooden building.
4. The veranda of the 19th century Shwe-in-bin monastery, in the eastern precinct of Mandalay. While it sits well back from the edge of the veranda there are broad windows which may be opened out to protect the interior against the sun and rain.

The Atumashi or "Incomparable" monastery lies just west of the Shwenandaw. This was the royal monastery built by King Mindon as one of the acts to found and consecrate the new capital. Instead of the usual tiers of the *pyat-that*, it has five graduated terraces making a large pyramid. It was built of teak and covered with an ornately sculpted layer of stucco. A disastrous fire in 1890 destroyed not only the building, but also the monastery's large image of the Buddha and four sets of the Buddhist canon, the *Tipitika*. For many years, the Atumashi remained a romantic ruin, but relatively recently it was restored to a new design.

The meritorious works of King Mindon also included the Maha-Lawka Marazein or Kuthodaw pagoda. The pagoda itself is said to be a replica of the rounded form of the 11th-century Shwezigon at Bagan. The Shwezigon, built by King Anawratha, is one of the most revered pagodas of Myanmar, as its construction commemorates Anawratha's proclamation of Theravada Buddhism as the official state religion and the banishment of the former *nat* worship.

In a similar declaration honouring Buddhism, King Mindon ordered 729 stone slabs inscribed with the entire *Tipitika* to be carved to form part of the Kuthodaw pagoda, as well as to occupy many of the small shrines around the main *zeidi*. They remain a valuable source of study for today's scholars.

The use of the Shwezigon as the architectural model for the Kuthodaw links Mandalay stylistically to Bagan. Mandalay's Shwekyimyint pagoda, however, dates to

the Bagan era. It was built by an exiled prince, Minshinsaw, son of the famous 12th-century King Alaungsithu. He installed an image of the Buddha that rests among many within the pagoda precinct. The Shwekyimyint is in the middle of present-day Mandalay, west of the palace. It is a richly endowed pagoda, with many images from royal families and a plethora of other shrines and donations.

In a pavilion at the back of the pagoda compound is an unusual reclining image of the Buddha. He is shown in a position of ease, his flowing robes painted a rich gold. However, rather than resting his head on his right arm, indicating his imminent ascent to Nirvana, his torso is upright. The figure sits upon a long throne or *palin*. Glittering glass mosaics cover the walls of the room created to shelter the image and arches over false doors replicate the wide half-circle curves seen over the doors at Mandalay palace. The room is separated from the rest of the interior by a beautifully executed wooden screen. Flowers and foliage twist and turn, creating a gold, lace-like effect.

The religious architecture of Mandalay is found at every turn. It is the result of the many donations of a royal capital, as well as an example of a centre of artistic activity. Monasteries, stupas and pagodas are located throughout the modern city and clustered at the base of Mandalay Hill. On the hill itself, shrines dot the slopes with covered stairs easing the task of ascending. Once the summit is reached, the pilgrim can look down to the wide moat surrounding the palace. To the west lie the blue shadows of the Shan Hills.

1. The small shrines of the Kuthodaw Pagoda, each sheltering a large slab inscribed with the *Tipitika*, the Buddhist canon.

2. and 3. A mass of slender, white-washed mini-stupas surround the Sandamuni pagoda, built on the site of King Mindon's temporary palace (where he lived while the Mandalay palace was being built). These small stupas house marble slabs inscribed with commentaries on the *Tipitika*. The shrines of Mandalay Hill can be seen in the distance.

1. The Shwedagon's main stupa rises 100 metres above the pagoda platform. Smaller stupas and single-celled shrines cluster at its foot. Images of the Buddha and guardian animals are found on eight planetary posts around the base, each associated with a direction and a day of the week. (Wednesday has two posts, one for morning and one for evening, making eight.) Above the base are the plinth, three square terraces, octagonal tiers, the bell, rings, lotus, banana bud, and *hti* (umbrella-like top of the stupa). At the summit is the golden orb, studded with more than 4,000 diamonds, one of 76 carats on its tip.

Shwedagon Pagoda

The Shwedagon pagoda is the most important shrine in Myanmar. The golden glow of its main stupa is an unforgettable sight, its smooth curves rising high into the rich blue of the tropical sky. Countless smaller *zeidis* and pavilions (*tazaung*) crowd the platform of the pagoda. Some hug the base of the central stupa while others are in remote corners of the platform on top of Singuttara hill. The platform—some 280 by 220 metres—was levelled more than 2,000 years ago, long before the founding of the city of Rangoon (present-day Yangon).

The legendary history of the Shwedagon puts its founding in the lifetime of the Buddha Gotama, the 6th century BC. Encased deep within it, there is said to be a golden barge, studded with jewels, in the form of a mythical bird, the *karaweik*. The golden vessel encloses eight sacred hairs of the Buddha apparently given to two merchants from Myanmar who journeyed to India.

The story goes that it was a time of famine and the brothers had travelled with a boatload of rice that they had placed on 500 ox-carts. The mother of the two brothers, Taphussa and Bhallika, had died and become a *nat*. She urged them to seek out the recently enlightened Buddha and receive his teaching. The brothers found the Buddha meditating, and offered him cakes of honey ornamented with golden flowers. When it was time for their departure, they begged the Buddha for a remembrance. He obliged, giving them eight hairs. They placed these in an emerald casket, and then into a *pyat-that* adorned with rubies. The brothers, after many adventures, arrived safely in Rangoon with the relics. A chamber was prepared and they were placed in a cave deep within the Shwedagon Hill.

An understanding of the Shwedagon begins with an acceptance of its legends and history. Both have been part of its sacred nature for over 2,000 years. It will never be known whether the relics indeed rest within the pagoda. In the 6th century BC, the delta area around the city was probably below water, with the Shwedagon's Singuttara Hill being one of the few elevated places. As such, the prehistoric occupants of the small fishing village that preceded the founding of Rangoon undoubtedly venerated the hill. Over centuries, the pagoda has been continually enlarged and repaired through donations by king and commoner. Royal donations traditionally equalled political sovereignty over the delta area.

The Shwedagon hill is north of the city's busiest section, the congested streets near the river front. There are four approaches to the Shwedagon at each of the cardinal directions, but the main entry is the long

staircase to the south. Today this opens on to a busy intersection, but it has always been the traditional entry because visitors in the past would have arrived at the city's port. The Shwedagon Pagoda Road is lined with monasteries (*kyaung*), rest houses (*zayat*) and other pagodas such as the Maha Vijaya just opposite the southern stair.

Before beginning the climb up to the pagoda platform, pilgrims and visitors pause to remove their shoes. Shops lining the stairs sell an endless variety of offerings, images and religious texts. At the top, the shade and cover of the stair opens out on to the smooth and wide esplanade that encircles the pagoda.

Everyone who visits the Shwedagon comes for a different reason. Some come to gaze upon what seems a magical world of golden forms, tinkling bells, and the quiet chants of those in prayer. Others, as pilgrims, come to the Shwedagon to make a ritual circuit, a circumnambulation. Some make this circuit to stop at nine wish-granting images, others to make an offering at their planetary post. There is no fixed pattern to a visit to the Shwedagon, just as there is no apparent "order" to the myriad of shrines on the pagoda platform. All contribute to its character, a unique and vital part of Myanmar's past and present.

1	3
2	4

1. A *pyat-that* marks the North Devotional *tazaung*, dedicated to the Buddha Gotama born in the 6th century BC. In addition to images of the Buddha Gotama, there are many images of previous Buddhas, guardians (*devas*), masters of the occult (*weizas*), and the territorial spirit or *nat* of the Shwedagon, the Bo Bo Gyi.
2. Daw Pwint's pavilion on the southwest part of the pagoda platform shelters a nine-metre long reclining figure of the Buddha. There are also images of his brother Ananda, and his two disciples Sariputta and Moggallana. Paintings recall the founding of the Kyaiktyo pagoda near Thaton.
3. The red roof tiles mark the *tazaung* of the north staircase. On the left is one of four iron figures of Indians in front of the Hall of the Buddha's footprint. Some call this the Venus pavilion, as this is the planet associated with the north. Slabs of black and white marble pave the pagoda platform, becoming warm in the noonday sun.

During the rains, however, the platform becomes smooth and slippery. Pilgrims, umbrellas aloft, walk slowly as they proceed around the *zeidi*.
4. A monk prays before golden images of the Buddha cast in bronze. Some images at the Shwedagon show the Buddha in a reclining position, but the overwhelming majority are in the *bhumisparsa mudra* or earth-touching posture seen here. The Buddha is depicted with his legs crossed, the soles of both feet up in the *padmasana* position. His left hand rests in his lap while the right reaches across his knee to touch the earth. It is perhaps the most significant of all the *mudras* as it recalls the moment when the Buddha defeated the forces of evil to gain enlightenment.
Overleaf. The curves of the Naung Daw Gyi or "Great Elder Brother" grace the northeast corner of the platform. The shape of this pagoda is said to preserve that of the central *zeidi* in previous centuries. The eight sacred hairs of the Buddha were first placed in the Naung Daw Gyi before being enshrined under the main pagoda. Small shrines, begging bowls (*thabeik*) or perhaps the *hintha* bird are found atop tall prayer-posts (*dagun-daing*).

ရ မြ နံ့ ေတာ် ကြီး ပုံ

က ရ ဝိက် ေပါင် ေတာ် ပုံ   အ ရှင် နန်း ေတာ် ဘု ရား သ ျှန် ေတာ် ပုံ

Secular Architecture

The religious monuments of Myanmar are world famous, and have comprised many studies. Secular architecture, on the other hand, has been sadly neglected. It is only fairly recently that vernacular architecture has begun to be seen to be worthy of examination. Indeed, it is now understood that to fully comprehend the ancient cities of Myannar, one must include a thorough examination of all the non-visible secular structures that once filled in the spaces between and beyond the religious monuments.

This is particularly true in the case of ancient Bagan. Although not built on the scale of Borobudur or Ankor Wat, the architecture of Bagan reached a degree of intricacy not found elsewhere. More than 2,000 brick and stone temples and stupas still stand scattered over a huge plain on the east bank of the Irrawaddy River. However, there is little extant evidence of the many secular structures that made up the living city.

Within the walled city lived the king, his royal court and a large community of monks. In fields, where ground peanuts now grow, once stood lavish royal palaces constructed completely of wood. And much like the dwelling of Indra on Mt Meru, the royal compound was sited in the centre of a square, raised masonry platform enclosed by four walls. Teak was the wood of choice because it was both widely available and strong. Master craftsman were employed to embellish the palaces with exquisite carvings and paintings. They strove to create spaces that resembled an abode fit for a god. The king's wooden thrones were carved to resemble the base of a Buddha statue in a temple, covered with silver and gold and embedded with gems and glass. Seated upon his throne within a huge vaulted gallery and entertained by dancers, singers and musicians, the king presided over a succession of rituals and festivals.

The remaining space was filled with monastery compounds and homes of lesser royalty and members of court. Monastery buildings served as living quarters and meditation realms for the resident monks who oversaw the activities of the temples and stupas. Though grand in scale, they were built more in the spirit of Buddhism's message of simplicity.

1. A beautifully rendered drawing on cloth of King Mindon's Mandalay palace. The palace has been compared to the dwelling of the god Indra upon Mt Meru. The royal barge sits anchored in the moat while soldiers stand guard before the tall brick wall of the palace. Courtesy of Beikthano Gallery,

Yangon.
2. The broad, vaulted roof lines of the summer palace of Myanmar's last monarch, King Thibaw, are accented with delicately carved gables and finials which lend a lofty elegance to the structure. Fabulous gardens spill into the open verandas surrounding the palace; the potted plants were an addition from colonial times. Private collection.
3. This archival photo of a traditional wood, bamboo and thatch Shan home clearly shows the three-tier aspects of a pile constructed house.

The homes of court members were simple compared to the king's palace, but it was a simplicity of law rather than one of faith. Although built of teak wood as the king's palace, strict laws governed the design and ornamentation of non-royal structures. The shapes of windows and doors, types and sizes of wood carvings, location of staircases, and various other architectural details were codified in an effort to reinforce the divine nature of the king. The opulent royal ceremonies and caste-like hierarchy of society were at odds with the tenets of Buddhism, which was the state religion. To rectify this contradiction, Hindu practices and rituals carried out by Brahmin priests were woven into the fabric of royal life. The design and layout of the city's architecture reflected the king's idealized concept of the natural and social order.

The architectural traditions of the Bagan kings were encoded in Pali inscriptions dating from the 12th century and carried over into future dynasties. Palaces were constructed of wood and built on raised rectangular terraces in the central enclosure. Because of the effects of climate, insects and fire in the tropics, wooden structures rarely survive more than 200 years. In addition, kings in Myanmar had a proclivity for relocating their capital cities, an activity that did not promote the preservation of palace structures. When King Mindon made the final relocation from Amarapura to Mandalay in 1856, he characteristically disassembled the royal palaces and used the wood to build his new palace compound in the new location. This final palace was destroyed by fire on 20 March 1945, by British shelling attempting to dislodge Japanese and Burmese soldiers. The few surviving wooden buildings, and the collections of paintings and numerous archival photographs, provide glimpses of the grandeur that these palaces once possessed.

In addition to these court structures were the houses of the people. Beyond the walls of Bagan, villages of farmers and fishermen stretched out to the horizon. Today—as then—the homes are elegant structures hoisted above the ground on a series of posts. What first catches the eye is the dominance of the roof as an architectural element. Steeply pitched and simply constructed, its pattern is repeated on all the homes of the village. A closer look shows a three-tiered structure built of wood, bamboo, and thatch, perhaps mirroring the realms of heaven, earth and hell.

This design has evolved over thousands of years as the movement of people throughout Southeast Asia lead to a sharing and mixing of building styles. It is believed that this pile construction (raised post technique) originated in Taiwan. The style spread south into the archipelago systems before making its way up the Malay Peninsula around 1,000 BC.

1. A traditionally built home in Sagaing where the under-storey space has been enclosed with removable wall panels that allow for seasonal temperature control indoors.

2. Louvered panels are raised above a small family food stand. These help keep the sun off the food.

3. A footbridge leads to a small home in Mandalay. His and her lavatories are sited in the back of the compound.

4. In this house teak window shutters allow light and air to pass into the home's interior. The second-storey veranda faces east.

5. King Mindon moved his capitol from Amarapura to Mandalay in 1857. The availability of water was an important factor in the move. Private collection.

6. Wooden siding and zinc roofs characterize these homes in Yaunghwe town. The cooler climate of Inle Lake has lead residents to select a more wind-proof building system.

Pile constructed buildings are raised above ground level by wood or bamboo posts normally two metres in height. In tropical environments, structures raised above ground level have many distinct advantages. They protect the inhabitants and their possessions from flooding caused by monsoon rains; the excellent under-floor ventilation helps cool the interior spaces; the piles protect the building from extensive rot and insect damage, especially when a hard wood is used, and an under-storey area is created which can serve as a protected area for animals or for storage.

The second level is where family activities are carried out. The location of specific areas inside the house is strictly regulated by tradition with a hierarchy based on gender and age. The interior is generally unlit as most livelihood activities are carried on outdoors.

The third tier is an attic like area. Here grain is stored for protection against rats and mould along with family heirlooms and valuables for protection and as a sign of respect. The roof, designed to protect everything below it, evolved from the earliest building forms in the region which were basically giant umbrellas. Steeply pitched roofs, now found on traditional homes in Myanmar, allow for the rapid runoff of intense seasonal rains. There is an opening between the roof and wall sections, which provides venting of cooking smoke and much needed cross ventilation. The roof is normally constructed of bamboo and thatch which lasts many years if properly installed and maintained.

The building materials are a perfect blend of form and function. Wood, bamboo, and thatch are all widely available and affordable. They have low thermal masses and transmit little heat into the living areas. The supports and roof wall sections can be easily lashed together allowing structures to be dismantled and reassembled in a new location.

The combination of materials and building techniques has produced an enduring style that is a delight to view and is ideally suited to the tropical climate and environment of Myanmar.

1. The homes of this large fishing village in Myanmar's Taninthayi Division (Tenasserim) are angled toward the water and heavily constructed to withstand typhoon-strength winds and wave surges. Photo by Jean-Léo Dugast, Photobank.

2. Since its earliest history, the plenitude of rivers in Myanmar has allowed its boat builders to prosper since its earliest history. Boats still provide an efficient and inexpensive means of transport between villages which line the banks of all the major waterways. Adaptations to the traditional pile construction home can be seen throughout the various climate zones of Myanmar.

3. In celebration of a young boy's initiation as a novice into the *Sangha* or monkhood, a *shin-pyu* ceremony winds its way through Myinkaba Village, Bagan. Just as one's clothes are not simply protection from the elements, architecture is not simply for shelter. Buildings are filled with symbols and messages that reflect and mould the world view of that culture. The differing roles of men and women, hierarchies of power, the interface between secular and religious life are all contained in the layout, structure and ornamentation of each and every building.

Village Houses of Bagan

Spectacular views of ancient stupas and temples can be observed from almost any point in Myinkaba, Minnanthu, Thiriyap and Tsaya, just a few of the small villages situated within Bagan's vast archaeological zone. In the same way that the dry desert air has preserved the past glory of Bagan's religious monuments, the villagers of Bagan have preserved the hospitality and gentle nature of earlier eras.

These people, mainly farmers of ground nuts and beans, weavers of cloth and baskets and masters in the art of lacquerware, continue with the same rhythms of life their ancestors followed. Time is measured here by cycles of crops and celestially regulated religious ceremonies. Buddhism permeates daily affairs, and an overriding sense of honesty surrounds relationships and personal interactions.

Their homes and villages exhibit the same straightforward and accessible characteristics, elegant yet unembellished. Materials are harvested locally and brought from the fields and markets by ox carts. Groups of men and women sit in the shade of giant ficus trees weaving slats of bamboo into wall panels or wrapping hand harvested grasses around lattice frames to form roof sections. Neighbours still come together to assist in house building and repairs.

| | 1 | | 2 | | 5 | |
| | | 3 | 4 | | 6 | |

1. People strolling down one of Minnanthu's many inter-connected lanes.
2. A group of homes shown clustered together beneath the branches of trees providing shade. Outdoor fires are not uncommon.
3. The crisp lines of this home clearly show the various roof and wall sections.
4. A woman uses a time-tested method to bring water from the well. This compound is enclosed with a fence of unforgiving cactus.
5. The water urns, oxen cart, and traditional home design can all be traced back in time to the era of the ancient stupas found all around.
6. Roofs of woven split bamboo reflect Bagan's hot afternoon sun. The light building materials of the homes and the shade provided by well-established trees help moderate the desert's extremes.

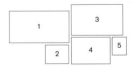

1. A baby nestled in a teak swing crib sleeps peacefully in her home's dark interior. Notice that the family's sleeping quarters are raised above the public area of the house.
2. A woman cleans rice in beautifully decorated lacquer baskets.
3. This collection of photographs chronicles the highlights of four generations. Respect for elders and an appreciation of their wisdom is still strong among the people of Bagan.
4. The open space between the roof line and the wall sections allows smoke to flow out of the house and encourages cool air to enter during the day.
5. A view of a roofing panel from below shows the wood framing over which the thatch layers are secured.

Mandalay Palace

The Mandalay palace was conceived and constructed during the reign of King Mindon who took the throne in a bloodless coup following the Second Anglo-Burmese war in 1852. At that time the royal city was in Amarapura which was built in 1782. The city's past was filled with royal intrigues and atrocities and this, combined with the recent humiliation of defeat to the British, drove King Mindon to seek a fresh site for his capital.

Seizing upon a fabricated prophecy that detailed the birth of a great Buddhist centre sited at the base of a great hill and on the 2,400 year anniversary of Gotama Buddha's death, King Mindon set out to build a "Golden City". He told his people that he had a vision in three dreams which required him to relocate his court to Mandalay. He felt the ruse was necessary because many of the 150,000 residents would experience great sacrifice and hardship in being forced to gather their possessions and follow the king.

After consultations with court astrologers, the most auspicious date was selected. On 13 February 1857, the first stone was placed in Mandalay. Great care was taken to follow the rituals and layout of earlier royal cities. Many elements of the palace design can be traced back in time, past the early Bagan kings into ancient Chinese and Indian dynasties. The orien-

tation of buildings was extremely important since the east was seen as the most honourable point of the compass, the source of life; and the west was the direction of death, where all funeral processions would leave the palace through the west gate. It is rumoured that the tradition of performing human sacrifices was followed, with 52 men, women and children being buried below massive teak posts which were set in strategic points about the palace. The ghosts of the victims were thought to remain close to their point of death and provide protection for those living within. Construction was completed in 1859 and Myanmar's final royal city became fully occupied.

The city was a perfect square, measuring 6,666 feet (about 2,030 m) per side. The palace was placed exactly in the centre with its outer walls facing the cardinal points of the compass. Twelve gates lead

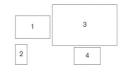

1. 1890s' photograph of people posing in front of the moat that surrounds the palace. The moat and double wall system of the palace were borrowed from ancient Indian and Chinese palace designs.
2. A *pyat-that* sits atop one of the corner gates of Mandalay palace. These towers were set upon all the gates of the palace, echoing a tradition described by Marco Polo while in Kublai Khan's palace in the 13th century.
3. The sun sets over the Mandalay palace. Covered with gold leaf and inlaid with coloured glass, the palace sparkles and glows in the bright tropical sun.
4. A royal barge in all its splendour and glory was moored on the west side of the moat in Mandalay and was used by the king in several annual ceremonies.
Plates 1, 2 and 4, and Plates 3, 4, 5, 7, 8 and 9 overleaf from a private collection.

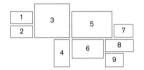

1. The central spire of the palace.
2. Gold-gilded, massive teak posts support the left Audience Hall.
3. A view of the Great Audience Hall and Central Spire.
4. All the buildings of the palace were only one storey in height. The number of roofs above a building indicates the importance of the area below.
5. Old photograph of the fantastic Lion Throne located in the Great Audience Hall. It was was one of eight thrones in the palace. When the British occupied the palace, they would have placed these potted plants here.
6. Concrete has replaced teak wood in the recent reconstruction of the Mandalay palace.
7. The 24-m Watch Tower, a spot from which to view the city.
8. Known as the Queen's Tea Room this building was in fact the Royal Guard Room.
9. The five-tiered Glass Palace was divided into two by a wooden partition. The east room contained the Bee Throne, which was embellished with carved bees, a good luck omen. The west room was the king's living room, and only he and his four main queens were allowed to sleep there.

into the city each marked with a different zodiac sign. Viewed from afar, it resembled the other worldly abode the king had sought to create.

The palace was dominated by a 78-m tall tower known as the "centre of the universe". This *pyat-that* tower had a seven-tiered roof structure that was completely gold plated. It rose directly above the Lion Throne and was supposed to be a great conduit for wisdom from above. The Lion Throne (*see pages 180–181*) resided in the Great Audience Hall where the most important ceremonies were conducted. *Kadaw* (paying homage ceremonies) were held three times a year with court officials and princes appearing before the king to swear an oath of loyalty.

All the structures of the palace were made of wood, much of it coming from the dismantled palace of Amarapura. Everything was carved with mythological creatures, floral designs and astrological symbols. A huge watchtower, from which guards scanned the city for fires, was constructed completely of teak and topped off with an exquisitely carved *pyat-that*.

King Mindon died in 1878 and, sadly, his Mandalay palace was completely destroyed by fire in 1945. A recent government reconstruction of the palace is an ongoing project.

Vernacular Architecture of Inle Lake

Inle Lake is a wonderland of natural beauty. It is long, thin and shallow and enclosed on two sides by hills of the Shan Plateau. Its nutrient-rich waters support a profusion of floating water hyacinths and cultivated gardens, while a bounty of fish thrive in its depths. The principal inhabitants are the Angsa or Intha, a Buddhist minority group. Known as "the children of the lake", it is believed that they migrated north in ancient times from the Taninthayi region (Tenasserim). Over time, they have prospered and now inhabit over 200 settlements.

The Intha villages are found both along the lake shores and directly in the lake. The water-bound villages are usually tightly clustered together and oriented in an east-west fashion. Homes are of a traditional post and beam construction with the structure raised well above the water on tall stilt-like posts. Walls are generally made of woven slats of bamboo, while the roof is composed of thatch.

The Intha utilize floating gardens, made from water hyacinths, marsh debris and soil, to grow flowers, fruits and vegetables year round. The gardens are secured to the bottom of the lake with long bamboo poles and are cultivated from boats, usually by the women of the village. Early morning markets are composed of buyers and sellers whose crafts are filled with colourful produce and who can be heard loudly negotiating from boat to boat.

The fisherman of Inle Lake are world famous for their one-legged rowing technique. The fisherman stands with one foot on the stern of the boat while wrapping the second leg around a long oar that he paddles in a slow circular stroke. Seeing a surface disturbance, he carefully navigates around the water hyacinths and throws a conical gill net trap into the water. Carp, catfish and eels are the catch of the day.

The Intha are a people who have adapted their particular brand of architecture and lifestyle perfectly to the enchanting environment.

1. Perched high above the water on long teak stilts, these Intha villagers' homes command a spectacular panorama of the Shan plateau. The stilts provide the homes with cool air circulation below floor level and a convenient place to tie up the family boat. The owners tumble out of bed into their boats and are practically at work.

2. This home in Ywama town is one of many Intha settlements located on the shores of Inle Lake. Due to a dramatic increase in development, future silting and pollution may severely impact the locals in the next few decades. The boat along the shore is of the type piloted by the one-legged rowers of the lake.
3. Lush, orderly gardens covering large areas of Inle Lake's surface take the first time visitor by surprise. The high yields and superior quality of produce from the lake's floating gardens enable farmers to sell their goods in markets as far away as Mandalay and Yangon.

Early Modern Architecture

By the end of a century of British presence in the country, very few of the local populace outside the cities had ever seen an Englishman. Public adminstration was largely staffed by Indian clerks, while most of the entrepreneurs and engineers who came seeking their fortunes were Scots. Yet, between the Second Anglo-Burmese War of 1852 and the end of World War II, the impact of the West was certainly felt by all in the rapid spread of roads, new ideas in building and urban planning, and a rich infusion of diverse decorative vocabularies.

Myanmar today retains more 19th- and early 20th-century architecture than any other country in Southeast Asia, though what is often refered to as "colonial architecture" was no more a single unifed style than it was purely a foreign aesthetic. An irrepressibly Asian love of ornamentation eagerly embraced the novelty of Victorian and Edwardian design idioms to create hybrid architectural forms as unique as the Anglo-Saracen monuments of India.

Outside of downtown Yangon, where Indian-built shophouses and public offices predominate, the numerous of most extant colonial-era buildings are Buddhist ordination halls (*thein*). Found throughout the country, these confections of moulded stucco with tiered roofs and stupa finials were donated by well-to-do Burmese merchants and rice-milling families affecting the latest "international standards" in sophistication, thereby enhancing their *kammic* merit as well as aiming to impress the community. After the 1880s and the abolition of the Konbaung Dynasty sumptuary laws (which forbad commoners from building large or ornate "palaces") brick-and-plaster with corrugated iron or zinc roofing became the building materials of choice, replacing teak, bamboo and palm thatch. Stone was seldom used; structures drew instead on centuries-old local traditions of solid-brick temple construction from Bagan and earlier, now adapted to the lighter columns, narrower walls and open arcades of Western-style villas.

The bricklayers may have been Burmese, but the plasterers were typically intinerant Indian journeymen who had no real grounding in the indigenous culture.

1. Carved teak rosette-boss on the main rotunda ceiling of the Karen Chapel, to the east of the Shwedagon Pagoda in Yangon.
2. Teak-shingled double-cupola with lace-like pendantives atop a minor monastery in the wooded Inya Myaing ("Golden Valley") residential area of Yangon.

As more and more splendiferous brick monasteries (*kyaung taik*) replaced older wooden temples, stucco decoration sometimes mimicked the traceries of Burmese *kanot* floral woodcarving; the odd door-frame or lintel might echo the ornate flourishes of Buddhist altar nimbuses. More often, however, stylistic inspiration derived from the neo-classicisms of Anglo-Indian mansions in Bengal. Façades concocted fanciful curries of Ionic and Corinthian pilasters and arched windows, scrolled corbels and keystones, sculpted festoons and baroque balustrades crested with the occasional Buddhistic peacock-hare "sun-moon" motif or *naga* serpent. Even British lions pay homage to the Buddha in the iconography of these temple halls!

Opinion among Myanmar's foreign residents toward such highly-mannered reworking of Europeanisms was not always favourable: "The old-style religious buildings were really beautiful—but the new-style *taik kyaungs* were hideous. So were most of the Burmese towns, but they were not Burmese in architecture and came from copying the West," wrote C J Richards in *The Burman: An Appreciation* (1853). Little did such East-West distinctions deter those wealthy and pious patrons to whom the rich new designs evoked realms beyond—both exotic and

otherworldly. And, by the 1930s, the *kyaung taik* was a well-established local tradition, no longer so very foreign at all.

Only slightly less prevalent in Myanmar are bungalows, those gentrified cottages that repose in rural towns, hill stations and former upper-class suburban estates such as Yangon's "Golden Valley" (present-day Inya Myaing). As suggested by the name, which originally derived from the Hindustani *bangala* meaning "hut", the basic bungalow form was transplanted from British India. As early as the 1830s, rather simple single-family homes raised on wooden posts or masonry piers began to appear, but here again the Burmese taste for embellishment soon took to the romanticism of cupolas and gabled roofs with "gingerbreaded" eave-line vergeboards, fretwork and pendants. Unlike India, there are virtually no large-scale manor houses in the country, yet the amount of detailing invested in these architectural gems make for some of the most delightful creations in the early-modern heritage of the country.

Finally, there are the three- and four-storey rowhouses that fill out the urban fabric of Yangon, Mawlamyaing (Moulmein) and other regional cities. Painted in pastel blues and yellows, whole blocks of profusely ornamented stucco facades—some spanning more than 100 metres—remain intact as nowhere else in Southeast Asia or even Calcutta. A few Chinese-style rooflines or carved doors evidence migration from the Straits Colonies in the 1920s; many more bear the Muslim names of Indian companies who built them as worker dormitories. Truly vernacular constructions, the architects and contractors are generally unknown. Most rowhouses, faded though still structurally sound, have been renovated and subdivided to house far larger communities than originally intended and cry out for conservation. These beautiful buildings are as alive as their bustling ground-floor shops and families that smile from their rococo balconies—endearing faces that stand witness to the changes occuring in Myanmar today.

1. The Boat Club on Kandawgyi (Royal Lake), Yangon, by the site of the Kandawgyi Palace Hotel. Along with the Gymkhana, it was one of the most popular expatriate social clubs of its day.
2. Deep eaves to shade against the tropical sun. Iron, zinc and tin roofing came from British Malaya.
3. A grand turret atop the former residence of Bogyoke Aung San, the father of Myanmar's independence movement, now a museum.
4. Old photograph of the interior of the bungalow of the manager of the Irrawaddy Flotilla Company, Yangon, *circa* 1880s, complete with wool carpet and upholstered chairs. The *punkah* fan-curtain draped from the ceiling made such warm furnishings acceptable in the tropics. Private collection.
5. One of the more ornate private residences hidden away in the garden estates of northwest Yangon.
Plates 1 and 4 from a private collection.

Old Rangoon

Yangon (as Rangoon is known today) retains little of the original Mon-Burman town of Dagon that once skirted the foot of the Shwedagon Pagoda. The city was entirely rebuilt after the Second Anglo-Burmese War of 1852, laid out on a long east-west grid by military engineers Fraser and Montgomerie and developed over the following decades by the Public Works Department and Bengal Corps of Engineers. The whole down-town port area had to be raised several feet for flood-control and modern sanitation, the Corporation of Rangoon raising funds by auctioning off private lots. By the turn of the century, Rangoon was reput-edly the most cosmopolitan city in the British Empire, with streetcars, gaslights and telephone services on a par with London.

The downtown area abounds in marvellous period architecture, both vernacular and landmark struc-tures. Among the most famous public buildings are the massive polychrome-brick High Court (1911) by James Ransome (1865–1944), Telegraph Office (1911) by John Begg (1866–1937) and citadel-like Secretariat (1905). The tower of the Port Authority (1920) stands at the head of the Pasodan (Phayre Street) main business district, still graced with the imposing façades of major banks and trading houses from the heyday of Rangoon's shipping industry. The Strand Hotel (1896), built by the Sarkies Brothers whose hotel chain included the famous Raffles Hotel in Singapore, has now been restored to its original splendour, though its view of the river remains blocked by recent port facilities. The most inspired examples of a syncretic Myanmar style are to be found in the tier-roofed Railway Station (1910) and City Hall (1927) designed by Burmese architect U Tin (1890–1972).

As the city grew, it pushed north into residential estates between Kandawgyi (Royal Lake) and Inya Lake (Lake Victoria). Nestled among the wooded lanes are fine examples of period architecture like the teak-spired Myoma High School (1922), also by U Tin, and the Dhammazedi (Boundary) Road arch-Victorian teak bungalows (circa 1920) of former Rangoon Mayor U Pa Thein. To its credit, as of 1996, the government established a listing of 71 heritage buildings, out of literally hundreds around Yangon. Now comes the challenge to implement preservation efforts to safeguard these sites for future generations.

District Courts, Strand Road, Rangoon.

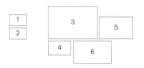

1 and 2. Proud lions and cherubic sculptural detailing on the façade of an Indian Merchant Association building tells of the past wealth of Yangon.

3. An orchestrated rhythm of arches, corbels and pilasters stratified between cornices on a shophouse façade in Yangon's Indian Quarter. Photo by Jean-Léo Dugast, Photobank.

4. The Port Authority, corner of Lower Pasodan and Strand, with its Spanish Mission-influenced carillon tower.

5. Period postcard of the District Courts (1911) by Public Works Department engineer Hoyne-Fox. The building later became the Headquarters of the Burma Socialist Programme Party.

6. A many-shuttered shophouse block in Yangon's Chinatown. Each building was allowed one narrow staircase for every 25 feet (8 m) of frontage. They are similar to Straits shophouses, if more massive in scale.

A Palladian Villa in Teak

This unlkely Buddhist retreat in southwest Mandalay was built in 1879 at the behest of U Kaung (1822–1908), a former Kinwun Mingyi (Minister of Foreign Affairs). He served as royal envoy to England and France in 1872 and 1874, where his duties included observing "things Western" both cultural and technological. Upon his return, he commissioned architects Comodo and Bonvallein, both formerly in the employ of King Mindon (r. 1853–78), to adapt European neo-classical style to a Burmese wooden building raised on stilts.

It is not known whether the construction was intended to be a villa or a monastic building, but it is thought that the Minister intended to retire here. However, at some point in time, the building became part of the nearby Thakawun or "Self-designated" monastery. Singularly quiet and understated, it is rectangular in plan and raised on masonry-footed pilings, as was traditional in Myanmar. Unlike most early modern monasteries, however, the Western-influenced forms here are rendered in the wood, not in brick and plaster; it is interesting to note how the woodworking and joinery echo the neo-classical composure of Palladio's villas (who in turn used stucco to emulate Roman stone architecture). The overall effect is planar and tableaux-like, each side repeating a graceful rhythm of pedimented windows and Ionic pillasters surmounted by a central gable.

The interior again features pedimented windows, together with delicate transom carvings over solid door-panels with fluted mouldings. A spiral staircase leads to a roof terrace, which formerly boasted a cupola over a central rotunda, now badly rain-damaged. The layout follows European models with its corridors and succession of individual rooms—more like private apartments than monks' quarters.

A rare late 19th-century Myanmar official reinterperation of Western taste in local materials, the Kinwun Mingyi villa stands as a counterpoint to the "entirely Burmese" Lieutenant-Governor's Residence (destroyed in World War II) that Lord Curzon had constructed inside the grounds of the Mandalay palace in demonstration of his keen interest in preserving the architectural traditions of Myanmar.

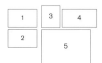

1. This large mansion is accessed by two large, whitewashed brick and plaster staircases, similar to the those that lead to traditional monasteries. There used to be a wooden balcony all around the building; this has now collapsed and been dismantled, thus explaining the whimsical appearance of the staircase that falls slightly short of the entrance.
2. The rotunda, in neo-classical style with Corinthian capitals on the top of the building, was once the centrepiece of an Italianate rooftop garden. It is now hidden below a roof hastily erected to protect the edifice from the vagaries of the tropical climate.
3. Richly carved, renaissance-style solid teak doors with floral detailing in the arched transoms lead from the main reception hall.
4. Although monks do not live here, an altar is set up in the hall on special Buddhist holidays and monks use the building.
5. The veranda at the front of the building is embellished by neo-classical windows and Victorian wooden gates. It now serves as an area for relaxation for the monks living in the large monastery compound.

Scottish Cottages in the Shan Hills

The old hill station of Maymyo (or "Maytown" after Colonel May of the Fifth Bengal Infantry Regiment) is a little Lake District in the Shan Hills just above Mandalay. Now called Pyin U Lwin, it boasts perhaps the most picturesque collection of colonial-era bungalows in the whole of Myanmar: over 100 former summer villas and estate houses of civil servants and private companies—mostly Scottish—but now owned by Chinese businessmen and military families, still survey gardens of roses and gladioli.

Today, the main street, a segment of the famous Burma Road, is lined with colourful souvenir shops run by a large Nepali community descended from Gurkha solidiers of the Raj. Two-storey shophouses boast well-preserved iron grillework balconies, intricately carved slat vergeboards and even chimneys. In the centre of town stands the Purcell Tower, erected in 1910 as a gift from Queen Victoria. The clock in the tower still chimes like Big Ben, although capped with a Burmese-style roof similar to that of Mandalay's royal Zegyo Clocktower (1903).

The Candacraig (Thiri Myaing) Hotel, built in 1906 as a chummery (bachelor quarters) for the Bombay-Burmah Trading Company, is surely the most striking extant period building. Posed on a hilltop by the Botanical Gardens, the brick and teak miniature manor house seems all the more imposing for its octagonal turrets and ivy-covered walls. Renovations may have tarnished its authenticity, but the entry hall with its lyre-shaped staircase has lost none of its charm.

1. Colonials escaped the heat and spent the summer months amidst Maymyo's gardens and fruit orchards. This photograph depicts a typical civil servant family bungalow.
2. Whitewashed turrets peer over the misty knolls. A former company lodge evokes an era long past.

1. The brick and teak Candacraig Hotel has changed little since colonial days. Unique to Maymyo, picturesque miniature horse carriages still ply the country roads.
2. A rustic woodland estate, just like home, back in Scotland.
3. A simple Edwardian-vintage vacation cottage with deep eaves and central chimney.
4. The entrance hall of the Candacraig with its staircase leading to the upper landing, parlour and guest rooms.

1930s' Monasteries at Sagaing

Some of the finest examples of brick and plaster temple halls (*kyaung taik*) are found in Sagaing, a major craft and religious centre across the river from Mandalay. A one-time Shan capital, Sagaing today is renowned for gold- and silver-smithing, as well as for housing the largest community of Buddhist nuns in the world. They live in many of the sanctuaries that dot the large steep hill, likewise famous for its breathtaking panorama of the Irrawaddy River. Sight-seers and pilgrims pack picnic lunches and spend the afternoon wandering from temple to temple amidst the flowering jacaranda trees along the ridge.

Around the base of Sagaing Hill, however, survive a number of very beautiful, but overlooked, colonial-influenced monasteries from the 1930s. Now sadly in varying degrees of disrepair, their elevated pediments and tiered jack-roofs exemplify early-modern Burmese syncretism at its peak. Typically Italianate in conception, the vertical proportions are accentuated in rhythms of tall, inter-columnated window arches and multiple cornices. However, the flat roofs fringed by raised parapet trimmings and balustrades also support pagoda spires and Buddhist statuary—heavenly *devas* or sphinx-like *manuthiha* whose double haunches spread perpendicularly in two directions around corners. Grand staircases mount the raised foundation platforms, playing up the solemnity of monastic processionals.

The interiors are often very spare, belying the rich façades; high-ceiling teak beams and mouldings—which once complemented chandeliers—hide behind cobwebs, as if in back-handed dismissal of worldly show. After decades of use, makeshift living quarters are still roped off with blankets and old robes. Faded calendars and dusty photos of past abbots are tacked up on the walls. Donated clocks chime at odd intervals. Despite the pride of the original patrons, the temples themselves have become time-less meditations on *vanitas*.

1 | 2

1. A triumphant peacock, sun-symbol of the Konbaung kings, crests the ornate stucco façade of a monastery in Sagaing.
2. A colourful Italianate façade further uplifted by tiered teak roofs.

1. A heavily-moulded late-
Renaissance balustrade ascends
to a monastery terrace.
2. Buddhist stupa finials and figures surmount the parapet of a
Portuguese-influenced façade. In
the past, when monasteries were
the sole responsibility of the
Burmese kings, their upkeep and
the monks' living expenses would
have been taken care of. After
the fall of the monarchy, when it
became feasible for the new rich
seeking merit to sponsor the
building of monasteries, it was
often simply the construction that
was paid for. In some cases, only
a façade was built! This is very
evident in Sagaing, where many
monasteries are empty shells,
mere ceremonial structures–
unused and falling into disrepair.

A Wonderland in Monywa

Eleven kilometres southeast of Monywa, a commercial centre of Upper Myanmar located a day-trip away from Mandalay, one finds the eclectic temple complex of Mohnin Thamboddhe pagoda. Composed of several buildings, all sponsored by various people seeking merit, the most strikingly bizarre edifice here is the Eng Aung Tong "Eternal Peace Hall". It was built in 1938 as an infirmary for the Buddhist *Sangha* by nouveau riche Singapore-Chinese medicine magnates Aw Boon Haw and Aw Boon Par for their spiritual mentor, the Mohnin Sayadaw U Kyauk Lon. A sort of "Hong Kong Tiger Gardens done up in Victoriana", it is now in a state of some disrepair

Enter though a triumphal arch flanked by two huge white elephant statues, and the tiger-topped gateway of this lavishly detailed "Tiger Dispensary" is on the right. Polychrome sculptural detailing abounds: every Corinthian capital has its little tiger; Kwan-yin, the Mahayana Goddess of Mercy, rides two dragons atop the façade. A colourful frieze celebrates the miraculous Buddha-blessed origins of Tiger-brand lotus balm; curious portrait figures of the illustrious Aw Brothers in modern suits attend at the entrance. A teak staircase with tiers of ascending gables extends from the rear of the dispensary, ornamented by cut-away traceries of leaping tigers and cornucopious bouquets.

1		
	2	6
3	4	5	7

1. *Trompe l'oeil* bunting and festoons above a doorframe.
2. **Main entrance to the monks' quarters.** Painted flower insets lighten the broad arches.
3. **A small *zeidi* with crowning *hti* complements the Victoriana.** Vines twine about the columns and yogi figures top the capitals.
4. **Slatwork traceries grace the gable over the rear staircase of the dispensary.**
5. **Butterfly and garland from a votive plaque.** Donor names are inscribed on their "good deed".
6. **A decorative door frame.**
7. **Stucco Buddhistic lotus petals and British roses on a minor *zeidi*.**

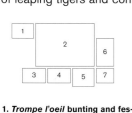

ဒါန သီလနှင့် သမထ ဝိပဿနာ မပါမူ သေခါကျမှ သိရလိမ့်မည်။

ကုန်မြို့

ဒေါ်မြကြည်၊ဒေါ်ရှုတင်၊

း ကြည်၊ ဒေါ်အေးကြည် တို့၏

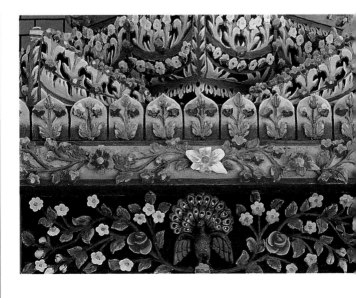

Inside, the long-vacant dispensary bears faded traces of a brilliant colour scheme. The ceiling wears a moulding of pastel-painted teak bats and butterflies, Chinese symbols of good fortune (not to mention a few live bats!). Tinted glass window-panes cast rainbows over the dusty wall-mounted alabaster Buddhas that watched over each bedstead. The overall effect is almost hallucinatory.

Indeed, the layout, replete with spiral view-tower, dainty gazebos and sculpture gardens, is more reminsicent of an amusement park than a place of worship. The giddy, festive flourishes, however, give way to a more sombre mood inside the main worship hall built from 1939 on by architect-astrologer U Han, after a premonition about the coming World War. Over a hundred thousand tiny Buddha statues stare from dark alcoves. Astrological symbols and hex-like diagrams posted at every turn render an arcane order that fuses Eastern cosmological mandala with British imperial pomp. The whole complex is truly a strange wonderment.

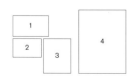

| 1 | | 4 |
| 2 | 3 | |

1. Frieze depicting the "miraculous" lotus balm cure. Here, a herbalist (*ziwaka*) administers to an ailing patient. Bounding tigers complete the image of vital energy.
2. Portrait bust of founder of the Aw Family fortunes, not quite identified by mock-Chinese characters.
3. Side view of the "Tiger Dispensary", complete with teak gabled window-awnings and tigers perched on the fence-posts.
4. A humble Aw Boon Haw welcomes the visitor to his flamboyant Eternal Peace Hall.

Contemporary Architecture

To speak of contemporary architecture in Myanmar is to speak of something newly born. Only in the last decade have contacts and investments from outside Myanmar been substantial enough to initiate a trend towards modernizing building designs, materials and construction techniques. Unfortunately much of the recent construction is disconnected from local cultural traditions and climatic and topographical realities. Those projects that have successfully blended traditional and modern elements provide an exciting glimpse of future possibilities.

One hundred and fifty years of British occupation in Myanmar have left a diverse and far-flung architectural legacy of grand brick and block colonial buildings. Though historically interesting, they provide little assistance in the development of a modern indigenous architecture. Existing religious and secular buildings, however, do provide a wealth of elements, both symbolic and practical. Construction materials such as wood, thatch and bamboo are climatically appropriate and easily available. In many village homes multi-tiered roofs, open verandas and courtyards integrate seamlessly with the requirements of modern tropical design. The aesthetic and symbolic qualities of Myanmar's Buddhist architectural traditions also provide a bridge connecting the community at large with the new forms that are beginning to redefine the local landscape.

In the forefront of this change, foreign investors are building new Western-style hotels and the local elite are building private homes. The successful projects all highlight similar points: Foremost is an appreciation and understanding of the environment into which the building is placed. Ensuring that the structure's design fits into the local topography and climate, and then tailoring construction techniques to minimize the impact upon the land, produces a harmony of place that one can instinctively sense. Taking advantage of the possibilities offered by local materials and utilizing the skills of Burmese craftsmen add to this harmony by balancing new forms with those found in the local architecture. Finally, architects that embrace cultural traditions with a sincerity that produces mutual respect and pride produce buildings that serve as an educational resource for local architects and builders alike.

1. A reflection of beauty and antiquity graces the surface of the pool found at the Novotel Mandalay which is situated to take full advantage of Mandalay Hill's temple-studded expanse. The sunset view here is truly awesome. Staggered white walls are used to both frame the background scene and provide a sense of privacy. The elaborate wooden resting pavilions were constructed to echo spires found in the Mandalay palace. The pavilions, receding towards Mandalay Hill, connect the two spaces and pull the background into the pool's setting.
2. An early evening view of the swimming pool in the Sedona Hotel, Yangon. The centerpiece of the pool is a delicately constructed "umbrella" which serves as both a sun shelter and light dining area. The pool is lined with multicoloured tiles in a swirling pattern that reinforces the organic curvature of the outline. Lush tropical gardens enclose the pool area. Silhouettes and shadows cast by the pavilion and surrounding foliage create a magical, dream-like scene.

A Renovated Mansion

Around 1920, the British colonial government constructed the Kayah Gayhar specifically to house visiting officials from the semi-autonomous Kayah (Karenni) State. Built entirely of Burmese teak, the two-storey structure admirably represents a classic phase of pre-independence Yangon architecture in which vernacular elements blended with colonial Victorian design to produce impressively proportioned villas. Many were private dwellings, others were used for official purposes.

The Kayah Gayhar made copious use of breezeways, high ceilings, elevated flooring and transomed walls to encourage air flows and cool living spaces in the hot, tropical weather. In its new role as a comfortable hotel called the Pansea Yangon, all of these elements, including the wooden grille-work along the verandas, have been preserved. In one of the most faithful restorations of a teak building carried out in Yangon in recent years, Patrick Robert has transformed the edifice while retaining much of the atmosphere and character of the original.

The Pansea's open ground design perfectly suits Yangon's year-round tropical climate. As the manager says: "We want our guests to feel some kind of contact with their surroundings, rather than being shut up in air-conditioned rectangles".

		2
	1	
		3

1. A dramatic, raised wooden walkway crosses a large pond added during restoration, emphasizing the hotel's cool, natural setting.

2. Custom-designed rattan ensembles, crafted entirely in Myanmar by the design company Traditions Co Ltd, furnish the voluminous upper terrace lounge. Of note are the restored teak-wood ceilings and floors.

3. Decorated with Burmese antiques and open to tropical breezes, the Pansea's restaurant maintains an elegantly local feel.

Rattan on the Lawn

Built in the lush setting of Yangon's Golden Valley, the late U Hla Maung designed a home that combined easy-going "California Living" with the British colonial style prevalent in the area. The exterior's flat, geometric surfaces are juxtaposed with a vegetative chorus of textures, shapes and colours.

Colonial-style rattan furniture and modern art intermingle throughout the interior with the tropical feel of potted plants and local handicrafts. The rooms with their large, lace-covered windows and high ceilings are light and airy. Treasures and keepsakes collected during travels for the Imperial Civil Service blend humour with grace and beauty. Late afternoons are spent seated comfortably outdoors in large rattan chairs. The second floor veranda's breakfast room looks out on the tree-lined front courtyard. The grounds and the home itself evoke both a nostalgia for things past and a feeling for possibilities of things yet to come.

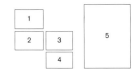

3 and 4. Rattan chairs and tables, made at the owners' furniture manufacturing and exporting factory, the Elephant House, are set out in the sunshine, the former on the lawn, the latter at the side of the house.
5. A powerful portrait of U Hla Maung's wife, Lucille, who is lovingly called "Auntie Lucie" by friends and family. The objects on her writing desk reveal both her serious and whimsical nature.

1. Afternoon light spills through lace curtains, enhancing the living room's relaxed colonial mood.
2. The dining room's geometric formality is softened with tropical textures and colours.

A Hotel by the Lake

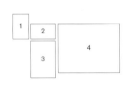

1. A wide veranda provides a space to sit and enjoy views of the lake. Concrete plinths supporting teak pillars and a woven thatch roof provide shelter from monsoon rains; these usually occur between 1:50 and 2:50 am all year round.
2. Sunrise on Royal Lake. A teak deck projects out over the lake, giving one the feeling of being on a boat. The glass objects and teak furniture are all produced in Yangon.
3. Whimsical towers shelter private dining pavilions which are provided for the hotel suites. The tiered roof form is reminiscent of spires (*pyat-that*) found on royal and religious buildings of the 18th and 19th century.
4. At the hotel's front lobby entrance, lofty teak pillars support a tiered roof system. The design anchors the hotel into the surrounding landscape and provides a wonderful transitional space for weary travellers who are making their way towards the lobby.

The Kandawgyi Palace Hotel, located on the south-western shore of Yangon's Royal Lake, is truly an illusion of place; an urban oasis. To the east stretches the lake's broad, calm surface. A serpentine shoreline, the banks of which are covered with a profusion of flowers, vines and trees, stretches to the horizon. To the west, a large stand of massive trees encircles the hotel, sheltering the entire area from the excessive heat of the late afternoon sun. At sunrise and sunset, flocks of birds crisscross the multicoloured waters of the lake, the sound of their wings clearly audible. It's hard to believe one is in central Yangon.

Most new construction in Yangon is done without regard for local architectural traditions or the land. However, throughout the design and building phases of this hotel, great effort was taken to preserve the existing environment and to integrate traditional building techniques and designs with the practical requirements of a contemporary luxury hotel. Completed in 1996 to a design by the Thai firm, Bunnag Architects, the result is a finely-crafted resort.

Design elements were selected from indigenous religious and secular buildings. Local craftsmen, utilizing local building materials, helped to connect the project to the community. The result is an excellent example of an alternative building design to the boxy, concrete block construction style sprouting up all over the city. It is hoped that it will influence the form of future developments and help carve a vocabulary of vernacular architecture that co-exists well with the climatic and cultural traditions of Myanmar.

An Echo from the Past

The Hotel Nikko Royal Lake Yangon is the first Japanese operated hotel in Yangon. It was designed by Thai architect, M L Tri Devakul of Tridhos Co Ltd, in a style that features spacious, open public areas. These gallery-like spaces are connected by wide, airy verandas and linear, walled walkways. Visual interest is provided by contrasts in texture. Rough exposed roof trusses are juxtaposed with sharp white support columns and broad, flat tile floors. Lush tropical foliage overlays wide, white walls and multi-tiered roof surfaces. The interplay between light and shadow has been displayed with great success. The repetition of forms and a careful balance between positive and negative elements has produced an especially calm, relaxing environment.

This balance extends further to the line between interior and exterior spaces. As you leave the interior areas, the wide verandas and terrace areas allow you to anticipate and flow easily into the gardens. The large, open interior spaces invite sounds and fragrances from the landscape to move inside. The huge windows provide a visual connection to the lakes and gardens from almost any point.

While the main building of the hotel is modern in style, traditional elements are found in both interior and exterior areas. Located in the gardens and terraces along the lakeshore, are resting and dining pavilions which are traditional in design and construction. The whitewashed walls surrounding the gardens, the walkways connecting the various outdoor spaces, and the serpent-like staircases are all reminiscent of similar structures found in local temple and monastery compounds. The hotel's gallery-like interior spaces are ideally suited to show off the exquisite hand-woven textiles, woodcarvings, and ceramic vessels produced by local artisans. The overall effect is one of simple elegance and understated beauty.

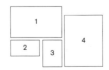

1. This pavilion's elegant roof system is supported by a series of sturdy whitewashed columns. The interplay of light and shadow, the texture of materials, and the ambiguity of being both indoors and outdoors creates a complex of emotions.
2. A sequence of differing lake views are framed by columns along the veranda. The repetition of forms in the columns, railings, shadows and urns provide a sense of balance and calm.
3. A *naga* **or serpent staircase leads from a water garden courtyard up to a resting pavilion. Changes in elevation have been used to form numerous private meditation areas.**
4. The garden walkways are designed much like a stepping-stone path in a classical Japanese tea garden. Changes in direction are used to frame important views and allow the observer to pause and look about.

A Bungalow by the River

Tucked into a secluded niche high above the east bank of Bagan's Irrawaddy River is Min Min Aung's magic bungalow. Harmony was the guiding force of this residence's design and construction. Traditional palm thatch and teak define a free-flowing space that has an animate spirit to it. Sited on the periphery of a 12th-century royal palace compound, the bungalow is as unassuming as the soil, stones and vegetation that surround it. To spend time here, one gains great respect for the ancient builders who chose this spot.

Here the movement of the sun directly affects the movement and mood of anyone inside the bungalow. Early morning shafts of light and gentle winds coax you from sleep and lead you to the thatch covered kitchen-dining area. As the light intensifies, the world expands exposing distant mountain ranges, gold-leafed stupas and boats starting their journey along the river. After breakfast, the focus of attention is moved to the west-facing veranda which looks out on the vast river basin. Afternoon's thick, heavy heat draws you into the shadows and the shelter of the lounge to read, relax and—certainly—nap. The movement of the shadows and the quickly changing colours of a Bagan sunset pull you outdoors. While seated with friends around the octagonal deck, glasses are filled and salutes are made to the day. As the sun slips behind the mountains, stars burst from the heavens while the silhouette of stupas and temples frame the horizon. Finally, a deep quiet slowly draws you into a bed draped with a misty canopy and you fall into a sleep of cosmic proportions. All is bliss.

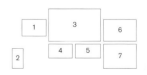

1. The deliberate blurring of the line between interior and exterior was accomplished by building verandas, decks and patios.
2. A *nat* shrine was placed here to appease any earth spirits

disturbed by the bungalow's construction.

3. The use of natural materials and a gradual fading out of man-made to natural spaces provides the house with an almost invisible presence.

4. The thatch roof of the veranda provides protection from sun and rain while still allowing for air movement. Shuttered windows and large louvered doors allow the walls to be almost deconstructed.

5. The teak octagonal deck encloses a black lacquered table. The post details on the deck are repeated in the brick wall along the cliff's edge.

6. Early morning light striking one of the outdoor sleeping nests. Siesta satisfaction is ensured by the prevailing breeze coming off the river.

7. Ancient clay meditation beads, local lacquerware and fine teak furniture match the harmony of the exterior.

Medieval Spaces in Bagan

Much of Aung Nyunt's childhood was spent exploring the myriad of ancient temples and stupas that dominate Bagan's landscape. His lifelong fascination and study of the building techniques, materials and forms of the era provided the inspiration for this riverside dining hall. The hall and outdoor plaza, built as a place to entertain large groups of friends and shelter guests in his garden restaurant from the monsoon rains, were completed in 1996.

Arch motifs and brick details mimic those found in the Kubyaukgyi temple in nearby Myinkaba village. The exterior shows an elegant blend of modern and traditional influences while the white wall and black-white tiles lighten the cavernous hall. Smooth lacquer and wood surfaces contrast with brick, bamboo and locally woven textiles. Archways and windows were laid out to frame garden views and highlight the collection of contemporary lacquerware and ceramics displayed there. The massive teak table and lacquer place settings are simple yet bold in design. Great attention was placed on balance and proportion. It is truly a grand space for a royal dining experience.

1. A broad tiered plaza leads from the hall to the river's edge while brick walkways wind through the garden areas. Almost one million handmade bricks were used in the construction of the hall and plaza.
2. In the background, the base of an ancient stupa is hidden by the west-facing façade of the dining hall. Aung's obsessive gardening habits have converted a former desert into an oasis.
3. Lacquerware from the family studio and water urns from northern Myanmar greet hungry guests entering the hall. The globe-shaped urn in the centre is a 19th-century treasure that was used to transport duck eggs.
4. Elegant brick archways, muted bamboo ceiling panels, rich teak wood, handmade lacquer food vessels, pewter utensils, the glassware–what a feast for the eyes! The table measures four metres by two metres and needs a group of eight to move it.

A Collector's Haven

In the quiet, leafy Yangon residential quarter known as Golden Valley, a designer of Asian furniture and handicrafts has restored and augmented the ruins of a colonial-era mansion to hold his growing collection of *objets d'art* from Myanmar and beyond.

It is a fitting retreat for a self-confessed culture hound who has spent much of his life assisting governments in cultural preservation and exploring those corners of the globe he found most stimulating. Burmese art has found its way into every corner of the house, but has often been re-interpreted to fit the forms and functions of modern Yangon living.

The two-storey house, constructed of triple-course brick in the 1930s as a private residence, sits on two acres of land and is surrounded by gardens of the current owner's design. The interior has been completely redesigned to encompass a dual-staircase, atrium foyer, spacious sitting areas, a glass-fronted dining room, a professional kitchen and six capacious bedrooms, each decorated with many unusual pieces of Asian art.

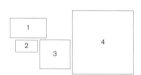

1. A corner of one of the guest rooms illuminates hardwood furniture designed by the owner's company Traditions Co Ltd in art-deco style. Upholstery fabrics are made of silk and cotton, hand-woven at Inle Lake in the Shan State.
2. A three-dimensional wooden relief *Jataka* panel dates from the early 20th century.
3. A small dining corner in the main living room decorated with a teakwood dining set of Chinese design, lacquered and polished. Many of the black lacquer pieces were made in the Kyaukka workshops, Chindwin District, at the turn of the century.
4. The owner's office contains custom-designed bookcases and a teakwood desk.

Many of the owners' ceramics originated in England or in the Netherlands and were specifically designed for the Southeast Asian market. Prominent firms were J and M O Bell & Co, who had a subsidiary in Yangon, the factory with the trademark "Bulloch" and two Dutch firms, Petrus Regout & Co and Société Céramique, both based in Maastricht.

1. At left and upper left, two earthenware plates by Bulloch, and that at the right probably by Petrus Regout & Co. The plate at the centre with the elephant design is unidentified.

2. The dining room features a chandelier made by the owner's company Traditions Co Ltd, inspired by the filigree work of a *hti*. The table is made of unpolished metal sheet, another item in the Traditions catalogue. The floor is covered with slate tile quarried in Kyaukse.

3. Earthenware plate created especially for the Myanmar trade by J & M P Bell, Glasgow, featuring the "Pegu" pattern: two kings engaged in combat on elephant-back with the broken parasol presumably indicating defeat.

4. Unidentified plate, probably of Dutch origin.

5. Earthenware water jugs designed for the South and Southeast Asian markets, one featuring a scene typical of the British Raj and another of a Burmese lady carrying a water pot on her head. Many variations on the latter theme appear on such water jugs. Another popular design is that of Queen Victoria's Jubilee.

6. Porcelain export wares of types highly prized by Straits Chinese. These include enamelled wares painted with phoenix-and-peony motifs against a wholly painted enamelled ground and having Buddhist/Taoist symbols on the borders, several types of blue and white wares, as well as a variety of the Straits Chinese *kamcheng* pot with a lion on the lid.

7. A potpourri of wares exported to Myanmar.

All the above wares are dated to the latter part of the 19th and early 20th century.

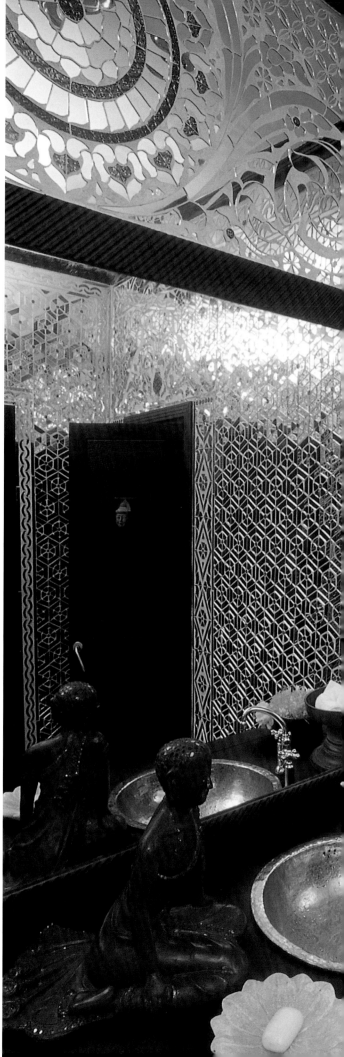

The house has become a protective showcase for Burmese art that might otherwise have been taken out of the country by foreign collectors. Amidst newer pieces of the owner's design, there are many antiques and handicrafts of local origin as well as European accessories brought to Myanmar during the colonial era. In another imaginative twist, pagoda ornamentation techniques, *pwe* drama themes, and more, have all been incorporated into the private living areas. In several areas of the house we see a combination of giltwork and reflective mosaic tile called *hman-si-shwe-cha*, traditionally one of the most popular ornamentation techniques in Mon and Burman temples.

As the owners, Patrick and Claudia Robert, say: "We've tried to create a place where we can experiment with Myanmar's Asian and Western heritages while retaining an overall sense of tradition."

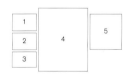

1. A Victorian-inspired four-poster bed readily accommodates mosquito netting.
2. The top of a locally crafted vanity adorns the edge of a terazzo tub.
3, 4, and 5. Reflective mosaic tile—designed, cut and assembled by a team of craftsmen from Mandalay—on washroom walls are reminiscent of Yangon's Botataung pagoda. Washbasins are made of hand-beaten brass plated with nickel.

Poolside Pavilions in Teak

Many of Yangon's residential lots contain well-maintained tropical gardens. When space permits, open-sided pavilions or *zayap* may be added so that the inhabitants can relax or entertain outdoors. *Zayap* traditionally serve as resting places for travellers or pilgrims, and consist of thatched or tiled roofs supported by rows of wood pillars. In this particular garden, there are three *zayap* set around a large swimming pool. Beneath them, one finds a plethora of teakwood furniture, all made by craftsmen employed by the company of the owners, Patrick and Claudia Robert. Called Traditions Co Ltd, it produces replicas of both vernacular and colonial designs, well-executed and beautifully finished.

1. Teakwood and wicker bench and chairs, replicas of colonial-style furniture favoured by the British and Dutch planters, beneath the main pavilion alongside the pool.
2. Victorian-inspired bench with sun motif is reflected in the azure waters of the large swimming pool.
3. Carved *bilu* (ogre) on left, Martaban jar at centre and two highly decorative chairs.
4. Built-in concrete benches beneath this *zayap* are covered in woven cotton from the Shan State. They provide a comfortable resting place for a quiet poolside drink.

A Country Gentleman's Mansion

When U Aung Nyunt set out to design his new home in 1996 there were three main concepts to integrate. He required a secure place to shelter and display his notable collection of antiques and local handicrafts. He wanted to employ only local craftsmen and use local building materials. Most importantly he hoped to provide a design alternative to the "modern" concrete and brick houses sprouting up in Bagan by highlighting the beauty and practicality of traditional construction techniques and motifs.

The traditional house in Myanmar is usually a three-tiered, wood pile construction. The ground floor serves as a space to shelter animals and its open nature allows air movement that cools the upper floors.

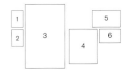

1. Gold-leaf covered teak hands in the "protection from danger by teaching" *mudra* adorn the study room door.
2. Black lacquered teak hands in the "protection from danger by giving" *mudra* grace the entrance to the reception room.
3. Showing off the natural beauty of teak and the exquisite workmanship of Aung's crew, this staircase leads to the home's private second storey. The stairs were built in angled form as evil spirits cannot turn corners easily.
4. The reception room provides a relaxed, open space to greet friends and share some of Bagan's strong, sweet tea. The integration of antique railings and wood carvings with the new wood construction is virtually seamless.
5. Two stone guardians watch over the first-floor entrance. The second-floor veranda provides spectacular views of Bagan's temples and countryside.
6. Delicate woodcarving in the form of a flower garland skirts the house, a symbol of hope and prosperity.

All personal activities are carried out on the second floor while the third floor is reserved for storing valuables, be it rice or family heirlooms. A prominent roof shields the house from heavy rains and the multi-level design allows for greater air circulation.

Aung modified this basic format to suit a more modern lifestyle. The ground floor serves as a public area containing the guest reception room, dining room, and kitchen. Tall, louvered doors open to allow for cooling during hot days; these are secured tightly at night.

Spaces of a more private nature are on the second floor. A large hand carved teak bed dominates the master bedroom. Encircled by astrological and floral carvings, the room's romantic feel is further enhanced by a pair of mythic half-bird, half-human lovers frozen in flight. The design studio is well insulated from the hustle and bustle of the first floor and features a window whose view frames a 12th-century ruin. The altar and meditation room is blessed with several magnificent Buddha images. Buddhist texts stored in manuscript cases and other ceremonial objects are used in various Buddhist rites.

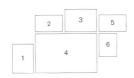

1. Handsome teak desk and chair in Aung's masculine study.
2. The kitchen was built in the traditional fashion preferred by Aung's wife Myint Myint Khin.
3. A limestone mortar for making *thanaka* powder. This natural cosmetic is popular country-wide.
4. The family altar is blessed each morning with fresh flowers and fruits. A 19th-century manuscript cabinet and other religious objects grace the meditation room.
5. Three clay water vessels await thirsty guests. A beautiful monk's table and set of coconut ladles complete the setting.
6. A pair of mythical lovers, the half-bird, half-human *kinnara* and *kinnari* float above the hand-carved master bed. Aung credits his success in life to the work he has accomplished with his hands and feet. He decided to honour them by having them carved on his bed posts.

A Princess Remembers

Daw Myint Myint Sein was born into a Shan royal family. Through the efforts of the head Shan *sawbwa* (prince), she was wedded to U Saw Khun Lee, a prince from Loicaw.

Both she and her husband travelled extensively throughout Myanmar. During their trips, Daw Myint Myint Sein collected many fine pieces of art. Following the death of her husband, she settled in Yangon to lead a quiet life and pursue her passion of studying and collecting art. Amongst her collections is an extensive display of Shan art. The Shan are famous for their silversmithing, laquerware, textile weaving and woodworking. Also well represented are arts and handicrafts from the rest of Myanmar, especially antique lacquerware.

A constant flow of friends, students and overseas guests arrive daily to experience Myint Myint Sein's gracious hospitality and the magnificent home she resides in.

The prayer room on the third floor is one of the most wondrous spaces one is likely to ever encounter. Upon entering, you are humbled by row after row of glowing images which emanate blessings and cheer—much like a field full of sunflowers leaning into the sun. A series of altars lines the east side of the

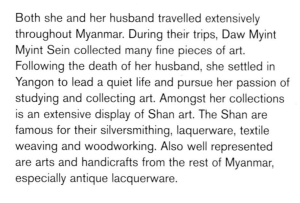

1. Although virtually all homes have an altar set up for them, volcanic Mt Popa is the true abode of Myanmar's 37 spirit *nats*. The small bags above the statues contain offerings to *nats* not present in statue form. Once a year Myint Myint Sein goes on a pilgrimage to present offerings to shrines dedicated to a specific *nat*.
2. A serene yet powerful Buddha alights atop a lotus blossom. Nine separate metals were blended to produce the warm colour and silky texture of this work of faith.
3. Silk banners and lace umbrellas float above a multitude of Buddha images. The bronze in the left foreground is a replica of the

famous Mahamuni image in Mandalay.
4. Treasured memories from Myint Myint Sein's youth. The meditation beads are symbolic of her devotion to Buddhism and the integration of the religious teachings into her daily activities.
5. Daw Myint Myint Sein is seated in her greeting room. Finely crafted silver bowls, huge ceramic vessels, and a friendly alabaster elephant are just a few of her eclectic objects. Dressed in traditional blouse and *longyi*, Myint Myint Sein's elegance and poise are mirrored throughout her home.
6. Novice monk image of Shin Upagok, with his right hand in his alms bowl and face tilted upwards. Several other novice monk figures are surrounded by royal regalia and chrysanthemums. The pavilion in the background is teak with gold-leaf appliqué.

room. Images of bronze, alabaster, wood and silver reveal moments and teachings from the life of the Buddha. The 37 *nats* of Myanmar's spirit world are represented in their entirety, each with a story, each with a special blessing. Flowers, fruits, lace umbrellas and coloured paper garlands fill the corners and frame the altars. Every region from the northern Himalayan mountains to the southern tropical zone is represented here. Prayer mats cover the floor below the altars and seated there, you experience the love and devotion felt by Myanmar's people towards their Buddhist religion.

1. An entourage of finely wrought bronze monks holding offering bowls. They were produced in the 18th century in northeastern Myanmar and display Chinese influences.

2. The main altar with a classic Shan Buddha seated at the summit where images, ranging in age from the 11th to 20th century and ranging from thumbnail size to over 15 cm in height, are blessed daily with offerings.

Arts and Crafts

Arts and crafts are synonymous with life in Myanmar. Life, in turn, is so closely intertwined with Buddhism that Buddhist devotion determines, in large part, the production of Burmese artisans and greatly influences their designs. Buddhism had become an integral part of Burmese life at least by the mid-fifth century of the first millennium: from that time onward, objects were created which reflect not only the superb craftsmanship of the artisans but also their fervent Buddhist beliefs.

This craftsmanship is based on a legacy of untold generations. Spectacular discoveries in the Pyadalin Caves comprise rock paintings, stone implements and cord-impressed pottery created about 11,000 years ago. In a report (*The Quaternary Stratigraphy and Palaeolithic-Neolithic Evidences from Central Burma*, University of Rangoon, 1985) on the investigation of some 31 archaeological sites in Central Myanmar, Thaw Tint and Sein Tun describe the discovery of a profusion of antiquities. These range from articles belonging to the Neolithic Age proper, to what they designate as the "metal age", and the early historical period. It determined that many present-day towns and villages, including well-known historical sites, are still situated in the same locations as Neolithic habitational clusters, some of which were nearly the same size as the modern settlements.

The authors found evidence of bronze metallurgical processing in at least five Neolithic sites in Central Myanmar, with the most developed in the lower Chindwin region (Mokhtaw, Aungtaung and Kyaukka) and around the volcanic areas (Songon–Mt Popa). From these, bronze knives, spearheads, axes or adzes and copper matte pieces were collected. In almost all the bronze sites, iron metallurgy and implements were also in evidence. This suggests that while bronze may have been produced earlier, iron and bronze were also produced together in what appears to be the late Neolithic era. A bronze hook, along with iron rods and knives, dated to about 460 BC, was found at Taungthaman (a site in modern Amarapura). Other items included bone or stone needles and spindle whorls, attesting to the existence of weaving skills and garment production at Neolithic settlements.

1

2

1. A typical example of the Burmese artisan's devotion to Buddhism, an antique manuscript cabinet embellished with a *shwe-zawa* (gold-leaf) design. At the centre is a kneeling *deva*, hands in a gesture of adoration holding lotuses in veneration of the Buddha; the whole is enriched by a wide convoluted lotus-leaf design. Courtesy of Patrick and Claudia Robert.
2. The *hsun-ok*, a Buddhist votive receptacle. The two here represent two aspects of Burmese art: one unadorned, yet noble, the other greatly embellished. From the Nunnery at Sagaing.

Dress and ornamentation, including jewellery, have always been important in Burmese culture. The presence of the court assured that materials would be finely woven, with appropriately regal designs. The *Manshu*, the 9th-century Chinese chronicle,describes Pyu women of Central Myanmar as wearing a high coiffure adorned with gold, silver and real pearls. Bagan was so rich during the reign of King Kyanzittha (r 1084–1113) that, in his great inscription at the Shwezigon pagoda, he declared that even poor people would wear golden ornaments and handsome clothes. Mon ceramic plaques of the 15th century bear figures of Mara's daughters wearing beautifully decorated *hta-meins* (wraparound skirts). Konbaung kings of the late 18th and 19th centuries made sure that royalty was clad in *lun-taya acheik* silk, time-consuming to weave and extremely intricate of design, in *pazun-zi* (cloth of gold and silver lace) and in both imported and palace-woven velvets. The laity were responsible for weaving the monks' robes, *kabalwe* (cloth covers for Buddhist manuscripts) and *sasigyo*, used to bind the *kabalwe*.

Manuscripts constituted an artwork in themselves, as well as being the bearers of important Buddhist texts. The decoration of *kammavaca*, manuscripts dedicated to extracts of the *Vinaya* (Discipline), involves lacquer design, while accordion-pleated mulberry paper manuscripts known as *parabaik*, often bear paintings which at times are related to the art of the murals.

When and where the art of lacquer came to Myanmar is still a matter of intense debate. The generic name for lacquer is *yun*, but this term also describes incised lacquer objects with themes mainly related to the *Jatakas*, the stories of the 547 lives of the Buddha prior to his birth as Prince Siddattha, court scenes, and local legends and tales. Other lacquer decorative techniques include *shwe-zawa* (gold leaf), *hman-zi shwe-cha* (glass inlay) and *thayo* (relief-moulded).

Many of the themes employed in lacquerware are related to those of the murals, of which the greatest early body in Southeast Asia is in Bagan. These murals, undoubtedly based on an earlier tradition of paintings which are no longer extant, completely filled the walls and vaults of the temples. Over the following centuries, the basic themes of the Bagan murals—the *Jatakas*, Footprints of the Buddha, Life of the Buddha and the 28 Buddhas which have thus far appeared—remained, but styles of presentation changed.

It can be assumed that complementary wood carvings existed, but only a few from early Bagan remain; the others date to the late 19th and early 20th centuries. However, the pre-eminence of Burmese woodcarvers goes unquestioned, as attested by a vast array of decorative and narrative masterpieces. These vary

1. Creativity with exactness and patience is demanded of artisans decorating *yun* incised lacquerware. Here, at U Aung Nyunt's workshop in Bagan, they apply an englobe of yellow lacquer to fill the etched lines of a design; thereafter, the excess lacquer will be removed.
2. Artisans examine the mould of a Buddha image which has been fired in a temporary kiln to melt the wax and to harden the clay for the reception of molten bronze.
3. A master sculpts in the specific details of the Buddha image's face after the second layer of malleable wax has been applied. After this, the image will be covered with two layers of clay, and prepared for casting.

from simple low relief, to the extremes of complex, three-dimensional specimens of high relief, to masterful carvings in the round. Entire monasteries and the Mandalay palace, tragically destroyed in World War II, testify to the outstanding skill of the Burmese woodworkers, whose competence, as is general in Myanmar, is wedded to and inspired by Buddhism.

Also related thematically to the murals of Bagan is a unique expression of the art of tapestry in the Burmese wall hangings known as *kalaga* ("Indian curtains"). These are distinctive for their sequinned and padded figures with sophisticated embroidery in stylized poses, illustrating the basic motifs of Buddhist art, and have become popular collector's items.

The temples of Bagan and Bago have long been known to be adorned with glazed plaques devoted largely to the *Jatakas* and portrayals of Mara's army. Only recently, however, have glazed ceramic wares—known to have been produced in Myanmar—been discovered. This discovery has opened a whole new field of study. Indeed, it has led to the realization on the part of art historians that there are still many unknowns about many of the arts and crafts in Myanmar.

For the world, however, undoubtedly the finest expression of Burmese art lies in the superb Buddha images created throughout the country and differing stylistically with periods of time and local preferences. Many

| 1 |

| 2 |

1. Artisans pour molten bronze from a crucible into one of two holes at the base of a large image mould placed upside down and suspended over a hole in the ground. They will continue to pour into the one hole until bronze comes out the other. A second image mould awaits the same process. To the rear are images in the wax stage, the second stage in the

making of a mould.
2. After the the outside layer and the inner clay core are crushed with the hammer, the eagerly awaited image of the Buddha is revealed. This one is a large image (seen at an earlier stage, Plate 3, previous page) and is at the stage prior to the removal of the holding rods, here nails. These nails are inserted into the core of the mould through its outer clay cover and the wax to keep everything secure. After the nails are removed, the image will be filled, filed and polished. Only then, will it be presented in its entirety for veneration at a temple compound.

would see those of bronze as the most important, especially those of late 11th- and early 12th-century Bagan. These result technically from a long tradition of bronze manufacture and from an equally long history of artistic sensitivity. Certainly the specially talented artisans of Myanmar have an aesthetic gift that is illustrated by a noteworthy artistic understanding as well as a refined skill in production.

Today the bronze manufacturing industry is centred in Mandalay's Tampawaddy quarter. Specifically in reference to casting a large Buddha image, a mould is made in three stages: Firstly, a mixture of red and ochre with rice husks, or yellow dust with horse manure, is pounded into a powder, and water is added to make a fine clay. The artist creates an image from this, delineating the proportions, posture, gesture, features and expressions. Secondly, the clay image is covered with an initial layer of wax which has been ground and flattened to make an even coating. Then a layer of more malleable wax is added on which specific details to appear on the finished image are sculpted. Finally, the wax image is covered with two layers of clay. While the clay is still soft, two holes are bored at the base of the image. Once the outer layer of the mould is hardened, the mould is placed in a temporary kiln of brick to melt the wax, which flows from the base, and to bake the mould for the reception of the bronze.

For casting Buddha images a compound of copper and zinc in the ratio of ten viss of copper (one viss equals 3.6 pounds) to eight of zinc is melted. The weighing and mixing is done by a master artisan. A large pit is dug deep enough to hold two red ochre crucibles, one on top of the other, each with a capacity to hold 40 to 50 viss of molten bronze. The fire underneath is fanned to a great heat. Pieces of coal are dropped into the topmost pot, and when it is sufficiently heated, copper is added, then zinc.

These are stirred with a bamboo ladle, and within minutes the copper and zinc dissolve and the mixture flows through the perforated bottom of the pot into the second pot below. The molten bronze is then ready to pour into one of the two large holes at the base of the mould, which has now been upturned to receive it. Before it is poured, a ladle of it is drawn to examine its texture and ascertain if it is wanting in copper. The bronze is poured into one hole until it comes out of the other. A day or two is needed for the bronze to cool and harden. Then the outside layer and the inner clay core are crushed with hammer blows. The resultant Buddha image may have dents or rough patches which need filling or filing down. Once this is done the master artisan uses a special iron rod with a pointed hook at the top to remove unwanted bits of bronze. The inner core is removed insofar as possible, and hands, ears or a crown which may have been cast separately are attached with bronze pins. Then the time-consuming filing and smoothing with petrified wood or another abrasive begins. Finally the image is polished with sesame oil.

Thus, we see here the existence of a union of faith, artistic genius and technical skill. It is no exaggeration to say that the arts and crafts of Myanmar have reached a degree of excellence rarely attained elsewhere in the world. Varying and developing from ancient times, through trials and successes, they now stand as examples of workmanship expressed with the brilliance and humility of the truly devout.

Bronzes

Burmese artisans are famous for casting immense bronze bells. The huge bell at Mingun commissioned by King Bodawpaya in 1790 is said to be the second largest in the world, with a height of four metres and a 5.3 m diameter. These bells play an important role in Buddhist devotions. They have no clapper and the exterior is struck with a length of wood by one who has made merit and wishes to pass it on to others to share.

The bronze used in casting a bell is composed of about 83% copper and 13% tin, a combination assuring sweetness of tone. Inscriptions on bells provide details about the donor, dating, the orthography of the period and more. Bells of inventive design and ornamentation were also made for cattle, and large bells were placed on the back of the lead oxen of caravans to keep the train in line.

Frog drums, so called because of the placing of frog images on their tympanum, have played an important role in rituals of the Karen minority since at least the 11th century. The prevailing styles are basically the same as those of the middle and late Ximeng type of drums used by the Wa and Dai people of Yunnan. Because of their popularity with foreign collectors, the drums are now produced in Tampawaddy (Mandalay), Yangon and Chiang Mai. The casting technique is consistent in general with the lost wax method used in casting Buddha images as described in the introduction. Ornamentation on the drums is provided by stamping the designs on the malleable wax layer during production by means of small metal dies. Handles and figures of small dimensions are made in separate moulds and applied later.

Among the small bronzes are the "opium weights" formerly used throughout Myanmar on one of the trays of a beam balance to determine the weight of the object of purchase. In sets of ten, the largest weight equalled 100 ticals (about 1,600 grams) and the smallest half a tical. They were stored with the scales in special carved boxes. The weights are often in the form of mythical birds or animals. The most common are the *hintha* (Brahmani duck), *karaweik* (Indian cuckoo) and *too* (a beast of part bull and part lion). Extant textual evidence indicates an initial 14th-century dating for the earliest weights.

	2	3
1		
	4	
	5	

1. The Maha Tissada bell, the Shwedagon pagoda, Yangon, cast in 1841, is suspended from a wooden crossbeam by supports in serpentine form. The top of the bell is decorated with a deer head and stylized figures of double-bodied lions with a human head.
2. A trapezoidal bronze cattle drum with elaborate raised design, early 20th century. Courtesy of Lopburi Arts and Antiques (Singapore).
3. Late 17th- to early 18th-century temple bell from U Aung Nyunt's collection in Bagan.
4. A Karen bronze drum with a star at the centre of the tympanum and four sets of three frogs, one upon the other, spaced equidistantly on its edge. The appearance of four sets of three frogs indicates a late dating in the sequence of drum manufacture. Courtesy of Rama Art, Bangkok.
5. Bronze opium weights in *karaweik* form, probably 19th century. Courtesy of Lopburi Arts and Antiques (Singapore).

Bagan Buddha Images

Bagan (Pagan) was at its height during the 11th–13th centuries, but continued to receive patronage from Burmese kings including the last monarch, Thibaw. The *Glass Palace Chronicle* places much emphasis on the fact that Bagan was initially a Pyu kingdom, and thus closely related to Thayekhittaya, Beikthano, Halin and other Pyu kingdoms in Central Myanmar in the first millennium. The inclusion of Pyu text in the Myazedi inscription, *circa* 1113, attests to their continued presence in Bagan.

The Pyu were great artisans. During the 5th century they were creating Gupta-style images of the Buddha in silver. By the 7th century, they were casting bronzes: examples include figures of musicians and dancers in the Pallava and Pandya styles of southern India, and a four-armed image of Avalokiteshvara with early Bihar influences from eastern India. Pyu bronzes, based later on Pala Dynasty models, continued to be cast well into the 11th century. While they were in the round, they were mainly to be viewed frontally, and often bore local features. Initially, the many stone images were sculpted in low relief, and later, under Pala influence, in increasingly high relief against a back-slab.

The first great king of Bagan, King Anawratha or Aniruddha (r. 1044–1077), created and inscribed with his name numerous votive tablets which he placed throughout his kingdom. These are of various designs, but all have at the centre a representation of the Buddha in *bhumisparsa mudra* within the Mahabodhi temple, Bodhgaya. The Buddha figures are stocky with broad shoulders, the faces large in proportion to the bodies, and—at times—with heads tilted forward suggesting a short neck.

1. The Buddha Kakusandha standing with hands in the *dhamma-cakka mudra*, the gesture of preaching the *Dhamma*. Wooden, lacquered and gilded, the Ananda temple, 9.5 m, early 12th century.
2. The Buddha in the *bhumis-parsa mudra*, the gesture of calling the earth to witness his good deeds in his previous lives; note the natural stance of the fingers. Late 11th–early 12th century. Courtesy of Lopburi Arts and Antiques (Singapore).
3. The Buddha's *Maha-parinirvana* (final death), Bagan Museum, *circa* the early 12th century. Brahma, Indra and other worshippers appear above.
4. Prince Siddhattha cuts his hair, symbolically severing his ties with the secular world, Bagan Museum, late 11th–early 12th century.

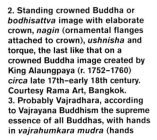

2. Standing crowned Buddha or *bodhisattva* image with elaborate crown, *nagin* (ornamental flanges attached to crown), *ushnisha* and torque, the last like that on a crowned Buddha image created by King Alaungpaya (r. 1752–1760) *circa* late 17th–early 18th century. Courtesy Rama Art, Bangkok.

3. Probably Vajradhara, according to Vajrayana Buddhism the supreme essence of all Buddhas, with hands in *vajrahumkara mudra* (hands

1. Wooden Buddha image with traces of red lacquer, low round *ushnisha*, left hand held high, palm facing inward, late 17th- early 18th century. Approx 2 m tall. Courtesy Rama Art, Bangkok.

Shortly before 1093, King Kyanzittha (r. 1084–1113) sent a mission to restore and endow the Mahabodhi temple. This resulted, for a brief period in the late 11th and early 12th centuries, in images influenced by Pala styles from southern Magadha (particularly in the Bodhgaya area). These often have attenuated bodies, as is the case with the two still extant standing Buddha images of the period at the centre of the Ananda temple: acquiline noses, broad shoulders, and in particular, thick thighs predominate. Heads continue to tilt forward and are large in proportion to the bodies. This, plus a puffiness in the waist, an unusually large *urna* (a whorl of hair between the brows emitting rays of light that illuminate the world) and very elongated earlobes differentiate them from Pala images. They are mostly in stela format, carved in high relief against a back-slab to be viewed frontally.

In the mid 12th century, a Burmanization of art began to take place. In murals, glosses in Burmese script were introduced and began to replace those in Mon. Buddha images became stouter and shorter, the faces broader and less acquiline, and the necks short. The faces still tilted forward, reminiscent of, but not the same as, those of Anawratha's reign.

Although the Bagan kingdom fell in the Mongol invasion of 1287, the creation of Buddha images continued and kept abreast stylistically with those in other parts of the country. By *circa* the 15th century, when Ava was the capital (First Ava Period, 1364–1555), the *ushnisha* (top-knot or fleshy protuberance, a mark of a superior being) had become centred on the head and was broader, with a small onion-shaped finial.

In the Bagan Museum, there are some 15th- and 16th-century crowned bronze images of Amitayus, the Buddha of Infinite Life, attesting to veneration there, as in Rakhine (Arakan) State. There is also, a 17th-century crowned image of Bhaisajyagura, the Buddha of Healing, stylistically similar to those of Rakhine and Shan States. In the 17th century, alabaster images of the Buddha Gotama became popular. These had a sweet smile and an onion-shaped finial larger and taller that those of the 15th-century; these are related stylistically to Shan State Buddha images.

Numerous crowned wooden images have been found in Bagan and Sa-le to the south. Both they and uncrowned wooden images have the right hand in the *varada mudra* (gesture of bestowing gifts) and the left hand held high, palm facing inward. This type of crowned image has been called Jambupati after what is considered to be an apocryphal Buddhist text of Southeast Asian origin (possibly Mon, as it does not appear in Sri Lanka or the northern countries of Buddhism). It is thought to have been invented by

Theravadins to rationalize the crowned Buddha images which were appearing with great frequency. The text tells the story of how the Buddha turned himself into a *rajadhiraja* (king of kings) to humble King Jambupati. Further study is necessary to resolve fully the identification of these wooden images. The pointed crowns and tall staff-like *ushnishas* relate them stylistically to the said 17th-century Bhaisajyaguru images. Thus, a date of the late 17th–early 18th century is suggested, during the Second Ava Period (1636–1752). In the following Konbaung period, the style of Bagan Buddha images mirrored those of the various capitals of the period.

crossed at the wrists in front of the chest and holding a *vajra* and bell, these missing here). *Circa late 17th–early 18th century. About 1 m tall. Courtesy of Daw Myint Myint Sein.*
4. Seated bronze Buddha image in *bhumisparsa mudra, circa* late 11th–early 12th century.
5. Standing Buddha image with right hand in *abhaya mudra*, a gesture of protection and reassurance, and left holding the edge of his robe. *circa* late 11th–early 12th century.
6. Typical late 11th–early 12th-century head of Buddha image with tight curls, *ushnisha* at back of head topped by a small lotus. Plates 4, 5 and 6 courtesy of Peng Seng Antiques, Bangkok.

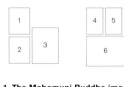

mental images in the region. Many are in the Arakan style as pictured on these pages.

2. Bronze image of the Buddha with right hand in *bhumisparsa mudra*, seated in *vajrasana* (diamond position). The lotus-bud finial and shape of the throne suggest an early 17th-century date.

3. Bronze image with 19th-century crown, Shwekyimyint pagoda, Mandalay.

4. Buddha image at the Eindawya pagoda, Mandalay.

5. Bronze Buddha image with high, broad *ushnisha* and the right hand in *bhumisparsa mudra*.

6. The Sandamuni Image, Mandalay, created by command of King Bodawpaya in 1802.

Plates 2 and 5 courtesy of Lopburi Arts and Antiques (Singapore).

1. The Mahamuni Buddha image, the most revered in Myanmar; bronze covered with a rich coating of gold leaf. The right hand is in the *bhumisparsa mudra*. Over the centuries, various Burmese kings tried unsuccessfully to bring the Mahamuni image to their capital. Finally, King Bodawpaya's invasion of Rakhine in 1784, resulted in it being conveyed to and installed in the Mahamuni (Hpayagyi) pagoda in Mandalay. Its presence there stimulated the creation of monu-

Rakhine Buddha Images

An ancient Rakhine (Arakan) manuscript, the Sappadanapakarana, relates that the Buddha Gotama came to Selagiri Hill; at the request of the Rakhine king, he had Thagyamin (Indra) and the divine architect Visvakarman, create an image in his likeness. This image, Mahamuni, was installed in a pagoda by that name at the city of Dhanyawadi, and Rakhine became known as "The Land of the Great Image".

Large pink sandstone plaques of *circa* the 5th century, found recently at Selagiri Hill and depicting in relief scenes from the Life of the Buddha, bear Gupta and Ajanta influence. Stelas of the same material and period at the Mahamuni pagoda, with *bodhisattvas* and other figures in relief, give evidence of Mahayana Buddhism in the area. A 10th-century terracotta votive tablet, now in the Mrauk-u Museum, shows the Buddha seated on a throne with rampant lions at each side. The Buddha's hair flows smoothly upward into the rounded *ushnisha*. The design is based on that of a 10th-century stone stela in eastern India and is like that on votive tablets in the Pyu and Mon areas. Thus Rakhine may have been a conduit for styles from India.

In the 15th to the late 16th century, Buddha images were corpulent with square faces, eyebrows meeting over downcast eyes, a wide, rounded *ushnisha*, no lotus finial, robes worn in the closed mode, and seated in *paryankasana* (one leg folded over the other) with the right hand in the *bhumisparsa mudra*. A bronze Buddha now in the same museum and dated to 1588 introduces a tiny flame at the top of the *ushnisha*. In the following century, the *ushnisha* and finial became larger and the throne waisted and filigreed.

The period from the 15th through the 17th century saw the development of the cult of Amitayus, Vajrayana Buddhism's esoteric Buddha of Infinite Life. His attribute is a vase of the elixir of immortality placed on his hands positioned in the *dhyana mudra* (meditation gesture). Early bronze images of the crowned Amitayus follow closely the Sino-Tibetan style of the Yong-le period (1403–1424). Later the facial features became more localized in appearance and the royal jewellery more elaborate. Around the 17th century, a new type of crowned Buddha image, which had a tall staff-like *ushnisha* and flamboyant *nagin* (ornamental flanges) at the crown's side, became popular. This style seems to have spread across the central area to the Shan State. Late in the century, images of Amitayus were created showing him with a tall crown of pointed leaves and seated on a throne flanked by what may be his two main *bodhisattvas*, and sometimes with the Earth Goddess on the base.

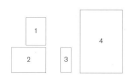

1. Wooden Buddha image with tall *ketumala* (aureole shown as a flame) seated in *paryankasana* (one leg folded over the other) against a back-slab shaped like a bodhi leaf, from the Kaw Gun Cave, *circa* 17th century. Courtesy of Galerie d'Art, Bangkok.
2. Also from the Kaw Gun Cave, three wooden Buddha images wearing tiered crowns and royal jewellery, *circa* 17th century. Courtesy of Galerie d'Art, Bangkok.
3. Bronze standing image of the Buddha, with missing hands, plus belting and central fold of the *antaravasaka*. Possibly 11th century. Courtesy of Lopburi Arts and Antiques, Singapore.
4. Standing image of the Buddha with robe having a four-petaled design indicating the Four Noble Truths, right hand in the *vitarka* (teaching) *mudra* and the left in the *varada* (gift-bestowing) *circa* 17th century. Courtesy of Rama Art, Bangkok.

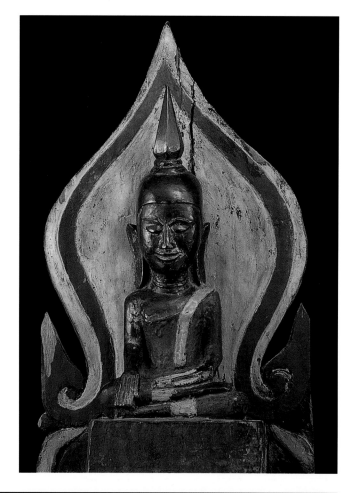

Mon Buddha Images

The Mons, scattered over southern Myanmar, have played an important role in Buddhist art since the mid first millennium. Plaques, plus statues of lions decorating the Kyontu pagoda near Waw, Bago District, attest to Mon veneration of the Buddha in about the 5th century and the influence of Gupta art. By the 7th–8th centuries, however, Mon images of the Buddha had become localized. They have plump faces with downcast eyes shaped like lotus petals, full lips, large hair curls, low *ushnishas* and long ears. Their robes were worn so that the bottom of the *uttarasanga* (the upper garment of a monk) formed the curve at the front and back, and the *antaravasaka* (undergarment) flowed below, as exemplified by two bronze images found at Thaton and Twante. In the 9th century the *ushnisha* became a high round knob, and in the following century it had the appearance of flowing upward seemingly from the hair to form a dome, as on Pyu Buddha images at Thayekhittaya (Srikshetra). Late 11th-century Pala influence is shown in two Buddha images on a votive tablet from the Kyaik De-ap pagoda (an old Mon pagoda in Yangon, destroyed during World War II).

A fragment and a Buddha image in the Shweizayan pagoda, Thaton, both with a *hintha* on each shoulder, have eyes downcast, a sweet smile, a narrow band on the forehead, and tight curls in a grid pattern terminating in a layered *ushnisha*; the *antaravasaka* has a belt and central fold. All the above are characteristics of Khmer Bayon art (late 12th–early 13th century), and probably result from the proximity of the great Bayon period Muang Singh complex.

Among large 15th-century ceramic plaques brought into Thailand from Bago is the glazed ceramic head of a youthful crowned Buddha image with high eyebrows over wide-open staring eyes. This style may have been the prototype for 17th-century crowned Buddha images imported into Thailand from the Kaw Gun Cave north of Moulmein (Mawlamyine).

With the crushing of the Mon kingdom in the mid 18th century, Mon influence in southern Myanmar waned.

1. The Buddha, who is supported by his disciples Moggallana and Sariputta, after he has fainted. Note the disciples' white, worried faces. Courtesy of Lopburi Arts and Antiques, Singapore.
2. Wooden standing Buddha of Healing with ornately decorated robe held back by his hands to form pleats at each side. Late 19th–early 20th century. Courtesy of Lopburi Arts and Antiques, Singapore.
3. Standing lacquered and gilded wooden Buddha image in the symmetrical attire of a Mandalay king with his right hand in *abhaya mudra*, *circa* 19th century. Victoria and Albert Museum, London.
4. Wooden seated Buddha images in *bhumisparsa mudra*, lacquered, inset with mirror glass and gilded. In front of the one to the viewer's left are two *lokanat*, originally thought to be a form of the *bodhisattva* Avalokiteshvara but now considered to be celestial beings revered by the world and noted for peacemaking. Shwedagon pagoda, late 19th century.
5. Lacquered wooden reclining Buddha with mirror glass inset on his forehead band and on his multi-folded robe. Courtesy of Lopburi Arts and Antiques, Singapore.

Mandalay Buddha Images

A youthful, sweet-faced image of the Buddha wearing a robe elaborately folded, edged and decorated, often with inset mirror glass, has attained great popularity and has become known as the "Mandalay Buddha". For many people, it came to epitomize the Burmese representation of the Buddha.

When Ava became the capital for the second time in 1634, Buddha images were often made of alabaster. These had an *ushnisha* shaped like a low truncated cone; a lotus-bud finial of onion shape; a narrow band between the forehead and hair; incised bow-shaped eyebrows, thin and raised; the nose with flaring nostrils; and a short upper lip, large chin and short neck. Images made of Kyaukse sandstone had faces similar to those of alabaster, but had diadems of an abbreviated form, related to those worn by crowned wooden Buddha images found in Bagan.

In 1753, King Alaungpaya had cast and placed in the Shwechettho pagoda, in his capital at Shwebo, a Buddha image with a tiered crown of jewelled lotus petals and large ornamental ear-flaps. Undoubtedly, it would have served as the prototype of the crowns of the Konbaung kings. The splendid torque of the image appears to derive from that of late 17th- to early 18th-century wooden Buddha images in Bago and Sa-le.

Late 18th-century–early 19th-century Buddha images in Central Myanmar had in many cases shed their onion-type lotus finial for one shaped like a pointed lotus bud. This is the case, for example, in the great alabaster Buddha image of the Kyauktawgyi pagoda, Amarapura, created by King Pagan Min in 1847. Yet in 1855, Linnaeus Tripe photographed in Amarapura a huge Buddha image of unprecedented Ava-Amarapura style. It had a broad *ushnisha*, no lotus finial and a more elaborate draping of the *uttarasanga* (outer robe) than usual. This may be based on the design of Rakhine Buddha images.

Mandalay images often have a broad band across the forehead. The hair hugs the head in tight curls and covers a broad prominent *ushnisha*. There is no lotus finial above. The images are frequently seated in *vajrasana* with the right hand in the *bhumisparsa mudra* and the left lying in the lap. The *uttarasanga* is worn in the open mode and the *sanghati* is folded decoratively on the left shoulder. Wood, alabaster and bronze have been the favoured materials. Many Buddha images are lacquered and gilded, including the face and body, the latter in accordance with the *suttas* (discourses of the Buddha) which relate that his complexion was like bronze, the colour of gold.

Most standing Buddha images wear the *uttarasanga* in the closed mode, covering the arms and chest and held at each side of the lower body by downward-stretched hands. Below, at its lower centre, appears the *antaravasaka*. The *sanghati* flows in multitudinous folds from the left shoulder. In his right hand the Buddha holds the medicinal myrobalan fruit. This suggests that the image is Bhaisajyaguru, a form of the Buddha of Healing, one of whose attributes is the myrobalan.

Although the above represents the prevalent style for standing Mandalay Buddha images, a notable image shown herein is attired differently, in royal costume similar to that worn by King Thibaw, the last reigning monarch (1878–1885).

Shan Buddha Images

The Shan, who call themselves Tai, form one section of the large Tai ethnic group which is now believed to have spread from Southeast China through Vietnam, Laos, Thailand, Myanmar and Assam. Shan legends indicate that they were already in the part of Myanmar which they still inhabit as early as the mid 6th century. The word "Shan" comes from the same root as Syam (Siam); in Bagan they were known as the Syam.

Although there is evidence of occupation by kings of Bagan in and north of the Nyaungshwe Valley in the southern part of the Shan State, extant Shan Buddha images appear to date only from the 17th century. They have triangular faces with a broad forehead, eyebrows arched high over narrowly opened eyes, a pointed nose with triangular nostrils, pursed thin lips, large and elongated ears, and short necks. They are often seated in *vajrasana* with hands in the *bhumisparsa mudra*. Seventeenth-century images may be placed on high, waisted lotus thrones and wear immensely tall crowns with flamboyant *nagin* (ear flanges).

Bhaisajyaguru, a Medicine Buddha of Esoteric Buddhism, was venerated in the 17th century, and according to Dr Than Tun's 1951 study of images in the Pindaya Caves, remained so until the end of the 19th century, with one image of Bhaisajyaguru bearing an inscription of King Bodawpaya (r. 1782–1819). Also popular was the image of the Buddha Gotama seated on a waisted lotus throne with a disciple perched on a lotus stem at each side. With the passing of the centuries the Buddha's lotus-bud finial became taller, his robes more highly decorated, and the ornaments of royalty more intricate.

Sylvia Fraser-Lu in *Burmese Lacquerware* (1995) indicates that Shan dry lacquer images may have been made in Monywa. First a clay image was shaped, coated with an ash paste, dried, and covered with a lacquer-impregnated cloth which in turn was coated with *thayo*. When the image was hard, the clay core was removed and the image was refined, polished and further decorated.

1. Dry lacquer Buddha image with large rounded *ushnisha*, bulbous high lotus-bud finial, seated in *vajrasana* in *bhumisparsa mudra*, with intricate designs on his robe, *circa* 19th century. Nga Phe kyaung, Ywama at Inle Lake.
2. Bronze Buddha image on a waisted throne with disciples Moggallana and Sariputta, *circa* late 17th century.
3. Bhaisajyaguru with right hand in *varada mudra* and holding a myrobalan fruit and a medicine bowl in the left, *circa* 17th century.
4. The Buddha Gotama seated on Indra's throne in the Tavatimsa realm, where he went to preach the *Abhidhamma*, part of the *Tipitika*. The throne is supported by the elephant Eravan and four horses. The introduction of the latter is most unusual. *Circa* late 17th–early 18th century.
5. Crowned Buddha image decorated with *hman-zi shwe-cha*, wearing the elaborate flanged crown of the Konbaung kings, *circa* 19th century. Plates 2 and 5 courtesy of Lopburi Arts and Antiques (Singapore). Plates 3 and 4 from Daw Myint Myint Sein's collection.

Woodcarving

The woodcarving of Myanmar is justly famous. Few woodcarvers in the world can match the technical skills of Burmese artisans in creating designs of great spontaneity, freedom and intricacy. These designs may first be drawn on paper, especially ones of great detail. The general outline is cut first with saw, chisel and axe; then an expert with years of experience (a master woodcarver) does the carving.

Myanmar's great forests must have provided a wealth of material for woodcarvers in the first millennium and before. While no carvings remain from that period, those on the wooden lintels above the main entrance to the hall and the entrance to the shrine of the late 11th-century Nagayon, Bagan, give evidence in their sophistication that they are the product of a long lineage of woodcarving. Small images of what may be *vidhyadhara* (celestial beings who have attained wisdom and magical powers and can fly through the air) are depicted as fast-moving figures within rondels inside lozenges and within ellipsoids, the interiors and exteriors of which are ornamented with delicately carved flowers and what may be clouds. Also of the same period was a wooden door found at the Shwe-zigon pagoda, still extant at the turn of the century, with carved panels of scrollwork, flowers, musicians and dancers all seated within beaded borders.

Presently the Buddhist edifices extant in Bagan are largely of brick. One hardly realizes that Bagan was originally a city filled with wooden structures, since the palaces and many of the monastic buildings would have been of timber. All except a very few of the latter, which are late, have perished. Many of the edifices had tiered spire-like roofs (*pyat-that*).

1. A monk kneels with his hands raised in the *anjali mudra*, gesture of respect and adulation. Courtesy of Mr and Mrs D Wills.
2. The *hsaung-ma-gyi* in the *pyat-that-hsaung* of the early 20th-century Bagaya *kyaung*, Ava (Inwa). Note the balustrade with an attractive juxtaposition of simply turned balusters, within a frame crowded with large bodhi leaves, peacocks in rondels and minute decorative elements in relief.

1. Doorway and carved pediment and pilasters, Shwe-in-bin monastery, Mandalay.
2. Scenes from the Maha-ummagga *Jataka* (No 546), the story of the sage Mahosadha, from the Yoe Soe monastery in Sa-le.
3. Two wooden figures serve as gong holders, each wearing his lower garment tucked up in breeches fashion as was done to show off thigh tattoos, and sporting a jaunty *gaung-baung*. Courtesy of Mr and Mrs D Wills.

These were reserved for monasteries, palaces, royal barges and carriages. Temple murals in the 12th-century Lokahteikpan and the *circa* 13th-century Chaukpaya-hlange, plus a red ochre sketch in the Hpayathonzu, also of 13th-century Bagan, all depict *pyat-that hsaung* (buildings with a tiered roof) with imposing *makara* pediments on each side and a many-tiered roof. The Chaukpayahlange shows that the roof tiers and the finial were heavily carved and were gilded.

By the early part of the 17th century, as witnessed by the designs of doorways at the Hpowindaung Caves, a great change had taken place in the reliefs decorating doorways and windows. The pediments were no longer outlined by the bodies of two *makaras* as in classical Bagan, but were decorated at the sides with *saing-baung*, ornamented elements in the form of haunches of a wild ox. Wooden door panels with door guardians in relief attest to the virtuosity of the local carvers. The murals of these caves depict great palaces adorned with carved *pyat-that* and pediments plus royal carriages each with a carved *pyat-that*. The 18th-century murals of Bagan indicate the continuation of architectural and woodcarving styles.

In the late 18th and early part of the 19th century, the capital see-sawed between Ava and Amarapura. When King Mindon changed the capital site from Amarapura to Mandalay in 1857, he dismantled the wooden palace buildings and restructured them at Mandalay. Thus the remarkable carvings remaining from the palace now seen at the Shwenandaw monastery in Mandalay may date to a pre-Mandalay period.

Jatakas, stories of the lives of Gotama Buddha prior to his birth as Prince Siddhattha, appear to have been known in Myanmar at least in the 5th century. This is evidenced by a large terracotta plaque in high relief from the Khin-ba mound, Thayekhittaya, identified as depicting an episode in the Mugapakkha (Temiya) *Jataka* (No 538). The last ten *Jatakas* depicting the last ten lives of the Buddha are a favourite subject of woodcarvers, ceramicists and painters alike. In fact, they have been the most popular stories depicted in Burmese art since at least the 11th century.

The Mon in southern Myanmar initially followed a recension of 550 *Jataka* stories. In the late 11th century, King Kyanzittha of Bagan adopted the Singhalese recension of 547, which has remained the standard one. Although *Jataka* plaques surely must have been carved of wood during the classical Bagan period and before, the earliest extant wooden ones date to the Konbaung Dynasty (1752–1885). The *Jataka* carvings at the Yoe Soe monastery in Sa-le reflect a growing interest in portraying the lives of the ordinary people as found in murals of the *Jatakas* in 18th- and early 19th-century Bagan, and in Western realism introduced later in the 19th century.

Figures that play an important role in Buddhism such as the Buddha's disciples, novices and the *lokanat* (possibly a form of the *bodhisattva* Avalokiteshvara) are often found in monasteries and nunneries. Carvings of these figures may adorn the walls of religious sites and palaces or may be free-standing, and are accepted as a natural part of the life of the faithful.

Other woodcarvings for devotional use include such examples as the earth goddess Wathundaye wringing the water from her hair, attesting to the Buddha's right to Enlightenment because of all the water he ritually poured when he performed good deeds in his previous lives; Shin Thiwali, a standing monk with bowl and fan who is the patron saint of travellers; Shin Upagok, a seated monk glancing upward with his right hand in his alms bowl, propitiated for good weather; Thurathati (Svarasvati) goddess of learning and the guardian of the Buddhist scriptures, seen riding a *hintha* with a book in her hand; and the *tangu-daing*, a tall flagstaff generally decorated with a *hintha* and a long streamer.

1. The once-gilded, intricately carved pediment and pilasters of a doorway of the Shwenandaw monastery, Mandalay, built from materials obtained from the dismantling of the quarters of King Mindon (r. 1853–1870) in the Mandalay palace. It constitutes evidence of the splendour of the carving once at the palace, now destroyed.

2. Gilded woodcarving of the Vessantara *Jataka* (No 547), Shwenandaw monastery. The magisterial woodcarver has managed to compress all the scenes into a small triangular area of exceptional intricacy, presenting the story beginning at the bottom right and ascending in boustrophedon fashion to the apex.

3. Wooden images of the two disciples of the Buddha, Sariputta and Moggallana. Nunnery at Sagaing, early 20th century.

4. The *lokanat*, believed to be either a form of Avalokiteshvara, revered as the protector of the world between the *Mahaparinirvana* of the Buddha Gotama and the coming of the Future Buddha, Metteya, or a celestial guardian figure; Shwenandaw monastery, Mandalay.

Other subjects in which Myanmar woodcarvers delight are the beings from Buddhist cosmology and the *nats*. According to this cosmology, at the four cardinal points of Mt Meru, the great mountain at the centre of the universe, there are four continents. The southernmost is Jambu, on which is the Himavanta mountain range and forest. In the latter dwell the *kinnara* and *kinnari*, he half-man and she half-woman respectively, and both half-bird. The *kinnara* (*on left*) is depicted in the symmetrical royal attire of the Mandalay period with the addition of a tall flanged crown. The wings and tail flutter delicately to his rear. The artist has created a sense of motion and beauty in what could have been a static figure.

Respect for *nats* is an inherent part of Burmese culture, and carvings of *nats* are frequently seen. They may be nature spirits, ones from mythology, or humans who have died unnatural deaths. Included among the last are those who constitute a pantheon of 37 *nats*. *Nats* are specifically carved to be placed on pagoda platforms and other Buddhist edifices. As spirits, they require propitiation, and are also regarded, like humans, as disciples of the Buddha.

What may be No 29 of these, the Gold Nawrahta *nat*, and No 15, Lady Bandylegs, appear at *centre right*. The former is correctly dressed in the robes of a prince since he was a prince of Ava who was thrown into the Irrawaddy River and drowned in 1502. His distinguishing attributes are a polo mallet in one hand and a ball on the other, both missing here. Lady Bandylegs, the sister of the royal tutor, No 14, was executed. Her distinguishing features are naturally her bandy legs, portrayed by the artist. No 14, Lord Grandfather of Mandalay (*far right*), was executed with his sister, although innocent of any crime. A distinguishing feature is his right hand outstretched with the thumb placed on the top joint of the forefinger.

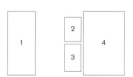

1. A *kinnara* with hands in the *anjali mudra*, *circa* late 19th–early 20th century.
2. Probably the Gold Nawrahta *nat*.
3. Probably Lady Bandylegs.
4. The Lord Grandfather of Mandalay.
All *nat* figures are of relief-moulded lacquer, gilded, with inset glass. All figures courtesy of Rama Art, Bangkok.

Stucco

Traditionally Myanmar's brick pagodas and temples have been embellished by a covering of gleaming white stucco with ornamentation by stucco in relief. The most prominent architectural feature is the flamboyant arched pediment which adorns the tops of doors and windows. The pediment is formed by stylized *makaras* (mythical sea animals), each with its head flaring outward at the base; the two bodies and tails in turn rise to create the arch.

Pediments became more attenuated as the height of buildings increased and appear in single, double or even triple form. Pediments, pilasters, and many other decorative architectural elements have a brick core which is ornamented with stucco reliefs. Many of these, especially repetitive motifs, are moulded. Ogres as guardian figures were a favourite theme; they appear in friezes on classical Bagan period edifices as heads disgorging bands of pearls which enclose floral pendants.

Architects through the centuries emulated early Bagan designs—albeit with variations. A great departure from this practice occurred in the 19th century with the presence of Western soldiers, diplomats, missionaries and traders: the result was Western architectural designs being incorporated into the traditional ones on Buddhist edifices. Paramount among these is the design of the Atumashi monastery, Mandalay, built during the reign of King Mindon in 1857.

1. **Stone perforated window with relief-moulded stucco decoration.** A *makara* pediment with a six-cusped arch is backed against tiers tapering to a stupa finial. Above is a frieze of ogre heads. Myinkaba Kubyaukgyi temple, Bagan, *circa* 1113.

2. **Painted bust of a crowned door guardian, stucco over brick core.** Ananda temple, Bagan, *circa* early 12th century.

3. **Small relief-moulded stucco ogres between stylized lotuses guard the Leidatgyi temple, Ava (Inwa), perhaps 18th century.**

4. **Pairs of elongated pediments adorn the entrances of the Maha Aungmye Bonzan monastery, Ava, early 19th century.**

5. **Stucco relief-moulded Italianate arches, base of the Atumashi monastery, Mandalay, 1857.**

Painting

1. Colossal ten-armed *bodhisattva*, outlined in red, with details in red and black against a red background. Myinkaba Kubyaukgyi temple, *circa* 1113.

Bagan (Pagan) contains the largest corpus of murals in Southeast Asia dating from the 11th to the 14th centuries. Pierre Pichard estimates that some 350 temples of the period still have mural paintings on their walls and under their vaults ("Sous les Voûtes de Pagan", *Ars Asiatiques*, XXVIII). Their beauty and perfection suggest the presence of a much earlier tradition of which nothing has survived.

Painting was employed for didactic purposes to present the essence of Buddhism to the faithful, but it also constituted an integral part of the architecture of each edifice, much in the same fashion as it does in renaissance and baroque Europe. An illusion of a much more elaborate architectural space was achieved by defining the space by means of decorative motifs (leaves, palmettes, rosettes, and so on), by dividing the scenes in registers, and by covering the entire surface of an interior, including the vault.

Jatakas, stories of the 547 lives of the Buddha prior to his being born as Prince Siddhattha, are the favourite subject, along with the Eight Grand Events in the Life of Buddha Gotama; the 28 previous Buddhas, including the Buddha Gotama, who have appeared in the various Buddhist cycles of time; Footprints of Buddhas; and myriads of Buddhas.

The paintings were applied *a secco* (to a dried wall surface). In the 11th and 12th centuries, the plaster applied to the brick walls was composed of a mixture of clay and sand with organic materials such as rice husks. This was given a final coating of fine slaked lime and allowed to dry. Areas were divided into grids by snapping cords, first horizontally and then vertically. Next an outline was made with a black or red pigment prior to painting. Pigments employed were white from lime, black from soot and fish gall, red from red ochre and cinnabar, yellow from orpiment, blue from copper sulphate and green from copper sulphate and orpiment. The powdered and ground pigments were mixed with water and an adhesive binder, probably a natural resin. Later, in the 13th–18th centuries, to ensure that the plaster would adhere, the brick walls were chipped. After the subjects were outlined, the colours were filled in and details added. Perspective was achieved not by use of the Western vanishing point, but by the relative positioning of the figures, such as by overlapping.

The style of painting in the 11th century was related to that of Pala India, but derived ultimately from Ajanta. Initially, the main paintings in the 11th-century temples such as the Nagayon and Pahtothamya were large. However, in the 12th century they became smaller and each of the 547 *Jatakas* was allocated a painting in a small rectangle. In the mid-12th century,

artists painting murals in the Lokahteikpan temple tried to rectify this in part by presenting episodes from each of the last ten *Jatakas* in strips or ribbons on the west wall of the hall.

According to the *Pagan Newsletter*, 4–7, (1988), a painting on cloth was discovered in Temple No 315 in 1984. It resembles the *Jataka* murals of the Lokahteikpan, with episodes painted in registers. Pigments used included cinnabar, lacquer, carbon black, orpiment, yellow and red ochre, copper green and black. This gives evidence that such paintings existed side by side with the temple murals. However, this style of painting *Jataka* episodes did not continue. In succeeding decades, paintings introduced an increasing number of mythological creatures which have affinities to Newari paintings in Nepal and Tibet.

Most of the murals are based on the Theravadin texts and are accompanied by a legend in ink. However, paintings in a few edifices can be seen to bear Mahayana and Vajrayana influences, the latter seen in the depiction of *bodhisattvas* with consorts.

Only a few fragments of paintings are extant between those of the classical Bagan period and the 17th century. Dating to *circa* the mid-17th century are those on the walls of the Hpowindaung Caves, west of the Chindwin River in the Monywa area, and to *circa* 1672 those in the Tilawkaguru Cave, Sagaing. The style of presentation is the same: the positioning of scenes from the *Jatakas* in strips or ribbons with scene dividers in the form of foliage, rocks and architectural elements. This harks back to the style first executed at the Lokahteikpan temple. While the

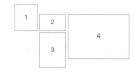

1. The *bodhisattva*, Avalokiteshvara, is seated in *lalitasana* (royal ease) with his left leg folded on the seat and his right pendent and resting on a lotus. This right hand is in the *varada mudra* (gesture of bestowing gifts) while his left holds a long-stemmed lotus. At each side appears an attendant. Abeyadana temple, Myinkaba, late 11th century.
2. Four of the 28 Buddhas with hands in the *dhammacakka mudra*, or gesture of preaching the *Dhamma*. Above each is the tree under which he became enlightened. Below, *devas* and humans rejoice at their enlightenment. Hpayathonzu temple, Minnanthu, *circa* 13th century.
3. A *bodhisattva* embraces his two consorts while holding a stemmed lotus in his right hand. A complementary design of lotus foliage decorates the frame. Hpayathonzu temple, Minnanthu, *circa* 13th century.
4. Sequential scenes from the ten last *Jatakas* decorate the west wall of the hall of the Lokahteikpan temple, *circa* mid-11th century.

1. Scenes from two *Jatakas*, Tilawkaguru Cave, Sagaing, with those of each *Jataka* placed on a separate strip, divided by architectural elements and foliage. The figures all wear distinctive headdresses, have the high arched eyebrows of the 17th century and wear large earrings; the men have what appears to be a quid of betel in one cheek.

2. The Buddha with his left hand in the *vitarka* (teaching) *mudra* stands within a *prabhamandala* (circle of light or radiance, an aura or halo radiating from the head or body) indicating transcendence or divinity. Thambula temple, Bagan, *circa* 13th century.

3. Turquoise brightens this mural showing the various business transactions of the Bodhisatta, born into a treasurer's family. *Jataka* No 4, Ananda *Okkyaung*, Bagan, *circa* 1776.

4. A part of a procession to the monastery presenting the methods of carrying food to the monks and the elegant dress of the 18th century. Sulamani temple, Bagan.

narrative styles of the *Jatakas* at the two cave complexes is the same and both are *a secco* in production, the style of the figures is different. Also, at the Hpowindaung Caves, the figures loom unexpectedly at times and some still-to-be explained themes appear.

Early 18th-century paintings in the Taungbi monastery and Yadana Myitzu pagoda, Bagan, closely resemble those of Tilawkaguru Cave in narrative style, size and colour.

The second largest extant corpus of murals dates to the Konbaung Dynasty (1752–1855) with many from the latter half of the 18th and early 19th century in Bagan. Numerous new Buddhist edifices were erected and traditional subjects painted, but with a fresh approach. *Jatakas*, by far the most popular subject, were no longer painted in long strips. Instead, the viewer looks down into buildings from on high; walls, stairways and courtyards are placed so as to give an illusion of depth, and provide areas for separate scenes. The narratives are further developed with several episodes presented and genre scenes are included which are not linked directly to the story.

1. A watercolour by Hsaya Chone and Hsaya Saw depicts King Thibaw at the centre, wearing his *salwe* (sash), and two of his ministers, the leftmost of whom seems to point to the British officers at the right, probably Colonel Sladen, the British representative, and an aide. Placed on the table are priceless rubies, the possession of which the British officer seems to ponder while his subordinate looks away. Courtesy of the Beikthano Gallery, Yangon.

2. A nouveau riche Burmese family in affected poses, wearing jewels and the *acheik* and velvet sandals formerly reserved for royalty, lounges on a European-style sofa. The wife holds up a naked baby for all to see and exposes her breasts, ready for nursing, in non-Burmese fashion, while the husband places his left leg over his right knee, the foot pointing outwards, in a manner deemed highly impolite in Burmese society. The painting may be by Hsaya Myo, since there is a similar one in the National Museum, Yangon. From the collection of Patrick and Claudia Robert.

Not only court life, but also that of the ordinary people in depicted, thus constituting a valuable cultural history of the period. A remarkable freedom characterizes the painters' styles, including their palettes. A favourite of some is a new bright turquoise.

The murals in the Kyauktawgyi pagoda in Amarapura, built in 1849 by King Pagan Min (r. 1846–1853), represent a new phase in painting. For the first time, they incorporate the linear and aerial perspective of Western art. The relationship of people and things is in correct scale and buildings and landscapes are convincingly presented.

Jane Terry Bailey points out that the artists have become acquainted with sfumato, chiaroscuro, three-point perspective and other aspects of Western art, and attributes this to what may have been Indians trained under British instructors, such as the Bengali artist Singey Bey, who accompanied Captain Michael Symes on his embassy to Inwa (Ava) in 1795. ("Some Burmese paintings of the 17th Century and Later, Part III", *Artibus Asiae*, 46).

In the late 19th and early 20th century, a small group of painters based in Mandalay turned to watercolour painting using Western perspective but depicting nationalistic themes. It included the artists Hsaya Chone, Hsaya Myo and Hsaya Saw and their pupils. Hsaya Chone is especially well known for two watercolours. One is of King Thibaw surrendering to General Harry Prendergast and Colonel Douglas Sladen in a summer house in the Mandalay palace gardens, and the other is of the king and his queen in a simple horse-drawn carriage, surrounded by rows of British soldiers, leaving Mandalay palace for exile. The Burmese bystanders are weeping. It seems that while they realize that Thibaw may not have been the best king, his departure meant the end of their country's independence.

Hsaya Myo and Hsaya Saw concentrated on family scenes (see right) in which they satirized the British way of life and lampooned those members of Burmese society who adopted British mannerisms and clothing and items previously reserved for royalty and members of the palace entourage.

Ceramics

The discovery in Pyadalin Cave, western Shan State, of a few cord-impressed shards among human bones dated to *circa* 11,000 years ago and stone implements regarded as belonging to the late Palaeolithic or early Neolithic period, indicates a long ceramic tradition in Myanmar. In *The Quaternary Stratigraphy and Palaeo-Neolithic Evidences from Central Burma* from 1985, Thaw Tint and Sein Tun state that the earliest pottery developed by the Neolithic peoples over the entire central part of Myanmar is an assemblage of rather coarse, dark pots. These have cord or mat-impressed designs on their surfaces and decorative cross-hatch and ridge-and-groove. During the late Neolithic phase, the potter's wheel was introduced, resulting in a group of creamy-gray pots of extremely fine texture and tremendous strength in spite of their relative thinness. Their surfaces were incised and stamped with geometric designs. At the same time, large container vessels–thick, smooth and burnished–were created. During the final Neolithic period in transition to the protohistoric, more frequent use of the potter's weeel and burnishing occurred, plus the introduction of red slipping. The wares have elaborate rims and pedestal bases. Related to these are the sophisticated wheel-turned, buff wares of Taungthaman, a site in Amarapura, dated to 460 BC. These were found associated with bronze and iron. Dr Thun Tun points out that a few of the wares were painted ("Pottery in Burma", *Mandalay Arts and Sciences University Annual,* 1972–73); this was with a red slip.

A plethora of unglazed wares for both ritualistic and domestic purposes has been found in first millennium Pyu cities, including Thayekhittaya, Beikthano and Halin. The most spectacular are large, wheel-turned, flanged funeral urns with flaring lids, decorated by paddling, rouletting and appliqué. These were excavated at Beikthano and were dated to the 1st–5th centuries by Aung Thaw (*The Excavation of Beikthano,* 1961).

Fifth-century, large, unglazed terracotta plaques with figures in relief have been discovered at the Khin-ba mound at Thayekhittaya and at the Kyontu pagoda at Waw, north of Bago. That the tradition continued is indicated by what are probably early 11th-century *Jataka* plaques on the Thagyapaya pagoda, Thaton.

To date, no early glazed wares have been found, even though the *Old Tang History* mentions a Pyu Kingdom with a city wall faced with glazed bricks, and the 9th-century *Manshu* adds "green bricks" and information that the Pyu brought glazed wares for barter. However, the sudden production in late 11th- and early 12th-century Bagan of large numbers of professionally produced, high-fired, earthenware lead-glazed plaques, glazed tiles and bricks give credence to the Chinese chronicles' statements. Also, fragments of plaques, dating to the same period, have been found in Bago.

1		4
	3	
2		

1. Green lead-glazed earthenware *Jataka* plaque with Old Burmese gloss, the Mingalazedi pagoda, Bagan. *Circa* 1277.

2. On three sides of the ground plinth of the Ananda, Bagan, plaques show soldiers of Mara's army marching in vain to prevent the Buddha's Enlightenment, and on the east side, as is the case here, celestial beings celebrate the Buddha's triumph. Green lead-glazed earthenware with Old Mon gloss. *Circa* early 12th century. About 45 cm square and 10 cm thick.

3. When his army failed, Mara sent his daughters to tempt the Buddha. Here, on a lead-glazed earthenware plaque from the Ajapala pagoda, *circa* 1472, two elegantly dressed daughters strike a suggestive pose; Hpayathonzu, south of Bago. Imported into Thailand from Myanmar in the mid-1980s. Courtesy of Lopburi Arts and Antiques (Singapore).

4. Two of Mara's warriors, here with human bodies and elephants' heads, dance in celebration of the Buddha's victory. Probably from the Shwegugyi pagoda, south of Bago. The large plaque is among the many ash-glazed stoneware ones imported into Thailand in the mid-1980s. Osothspha Ceramic Collection.

1. Martaban jar with reddish-orange slip and what is probably a lead glaze with iron colorant, tall body, short neck and two lugs. From the Tak/Omkoi finds, *circa* 15th–16th century. Osothspha Ceramic Collection.
2. Earthenware bottles with pinkish body and reddish-orange slip, covered in the upper portion with a green lead glaze. Two have striated paddle marks below. From the Tak/Omkoi finds, *circa* late 15th–early 16th century. Osothspha Ceramic Collection.
3. Earthenware lead-glazed bottle with iron colorant; vase with white slip over pinkish body, white and green lead glazes with tin and copper oxide colorants, sgraffito design in the green; and green lead-glazed bowl. From what was probably a kiln site at Sanka, Shan State. The bowl is influenced by a Guangdong design, *circa* 1880–1930. Private collection.
4. Earthenware bottles with a reddish slip over a pinkish body and a lead glaze given a creamy white opacity by tin oxide. From the Tak/Omkoi finds. *Circa* 15th–16th century. Private collection.
5. Earthenware plate with creamy white tin-opacified lead glaze and an in-glaze green floral motif at the centre and in the cavetto. From the Tak/Omkoi finds, 15th–16th century. Osothspha Ceramic Collection.

Plaques were covered with a green lead glaze with copper as the colorant and tin as the opacifier. The white, yellow and reds used in bricks and decorative elements were produced by tin, vanadium and iron oxides respectively. However, there is no definitive evidence that the technique originated there.

Thus far, six kilns have been found in the Myinkaba area of Bagan, all updraft and five very small. However, the smaller ones may have been used for glass-making. The lead glazing and the use of updraft kilns are similar to such techniques as originated in the Middle East by the Assyrians and were re-introduced in the 9th century. Chaw or *bwet*, not actually slag but an intermediate product of lead ore smelting, is powdered and mixed with water in which rice has been boiled. In both ancient and modern times, the resulting glaze was placed directly on dried wares, slipped or unslipped, and fired.

Bagan plaques were probably moulded, figures in relief luted on, dried, glaze applied and then fired. Much larger plaques than those at Bagan were once placed in the walls of the compound of the Shwegugyi pagoda and Ajapala pagoda, south of Bago, *circa* 1472. These vary in size and thickness and were probably cut from clay slabs. The figures in high relief were then luted on, the plaques dried, slipped, dried, glazed and fired. Both lead and ash glazes were used.

In and since 1984, finds in the Tak/Omkoi area of western Thailand have introduced many previously unknown high fired earthenware lead-glazed wares of Myanmar origin. They are white, red, brown, and white with an in-glaze green decoration. Production of the last may be similar to that of Majolica ware which began in the 15th century. Stonewares in the finds include celadons, ash-glazed and white-glazed wares. Large Martaban jars with what appears to be a brown lead glaze were also discovered. Kilns in two villages near Ava (Inwa), and a large crossdraft kiln that produced green glazed stoneware at the Mon village of Lagumbye, between Yangon and Bago, have been found. About 100 nearby kilns also all produced green-glazed stoneware. A group of kilns has been found at Myaung Mya in the Bassein area. Recently the remains of at least six kilns were discovered in Mrauk-U.

Collectors and ceramic lovers alike are eager to know which kilns produced the in-glazed green and white wares from Tak/Omkoi. It may be that they were produced at several sites, since the chaw from Bawzaing used in their manufacture was employed widely. It seems certain that one group of the green and white wares was produced in Mrauk-U, since in the local museum there is a fragment of tile bearing such a glaze which was made for the Jinamanaung pagoda built in Mrauk-U in 1652.

6. Celadon dish with deeply striated cavetto, flat rim with upturned edge, unglazed buff recessed base. Myanmar ware of Chinese Yuan Dynasty design. Late 13th–early 14th century. Private collection.

7. Ash-glazed stoneware storage jar with impressed design of *kalasa* pots and listening deer on the shoulder; high neck and flared mouth. The shape of the pot stems from the Middle East, *circa* late 13th–early 14th century. Jars of this type are in the Mrauk-U and Bagan Museums. Among the wares entering Thailand from Myanmar. Private collection.

8. A pair of lead-glazed *bilu* (ogre) bell bearers, Shwe-in-bin monastery, Mandalay, probably from a kiln in the Kyauk Myaung area above Mandalay. *Circa* 1895, when the monastery was commissioned.

1. A superb example of *yun* lacquer is this courting scene from a panel on a screen: A princess and her attendants meet a prince in the centre of a tree-filled arbour. The green of the trees is reflected in the garments. Late 19th/early 20th century.

2. Two different royal scenes are depicted in two horizontal bands on the cover of a large *yun*-lacquered chest. At the top a king watches a military parade with powerful elephants and a caparisoned horse. Below, another king's wedding is celebrated. Placing two parallel scenes on the cover of a large *yun*-lacquered chest is common.
3. Three court scenes enliven a chest. 20th century.
All pieces courtesy of Cherie Aung Khin, the Elephant House, Bangkok and Yangon.

Lacquerware

Among the great artistic achievements of the people of Myanmar is *yun*, the generic name for lacquer in Myanmar. Durable and beautiful items are produced by a time-tested method, the vital element of which is the sap from the *Melanorrhoea usitata* tree. First the object to be lacquered is constructed from either bamboo or wood. The lightest, most pliable lacquer wares are made of interwoven bamboo strips and horsehair. Other fine wares are made of woven and interlaced bamboo strips. Soft woods are used for screens, folding tables and rectangular boxes, and teak for heavier pieces. For bamboo, a dried bamboo trunk is cut into strips which may be coiled, woven or twisted as the shape of the object requires. When the basic form is completed, it is sealed by a coat of lacquer mixed with fine clay. It is then put into a special cellar to dry for three to ten days. Afterwards, it is smoothed and polished with pumice on a simple hand lathe, whereupon another and finer sealing layer is added and the object is put back into the cellar. This process is repeated again and again until the item is completely smooth. Finally, it is given a coat of fine, glossy-quality lacquer.

Several steps of sealing, polishing, drying and lacquering take place before an object is ready for final decoration. The lacquer which comes from the sap of the wild *Melanorrhoea* tree is naturally black. Different colours are produced with the addition of different elements: red by the addition of cinnabar, yellow by orpiment, blue by indigo, and green from a mixture of yellow and green. Blue was rarely used traditionally as a separate colour.

More precisely, the term *yun* is the name of a gloriously imaginative incised lacquerware. Here, the artist can show his capacity to bring legends to life and introduce a plethora of lively motifs. The style originated in China, and how it came to Myanmar and to be centred in Bagan is still debated. The technique demands skill and patience. An object already covered with a glossy coat of lacquer is incised sequentially with elements of an overall design to be presented in chosen colours. Supposing, for example, the background is black. The artist, working freehand, might first incise lines to be filled with red. The surface of the object is then entirely covered with the colorant, ensuring that the lines are also filled with red. It is then placed in a drying cellar for three or four days, after which the excess of red is removed by polishing on a lathe. The colour is sealed in by a coating of resin. When this is dry, the engraving of the second colour begins and the process continues through the next colour(s).

Kyaukka, in the lower Chindwin District, is responsible for many simple, but elegant lacquer articles for household and monastery use. Most are made from woven matting and coiled bamboo, lacquered black or red or a combination of the two. Some are clearly local in style. Prominent among them is a much sought after Kyaukka version of the *hsun-ok* (a votive receptacle).

Shwe-zawa (gold-leaf design lacquerware) is less time-consuming to produce than *yun* ware, but is just as demanding artistically. First, on a highly polished lacquer surface, the artist carefully blocks off the areas not to be gilded with a covering of orpiment and the gum of the neem tree. By so doing, he creates a negative design for the application of gold. Then a coat of fresh lacquer is placed on the blank areas and the entire surface of the object is covered with gold leaf. When the newly lacquered areas are almost dry, the surface is washed with water. Gold on the areas covered by orpiment is washed away, revealing a brilliant gold design on a shiny lacquer background. The object is then allowed to dry in a special cellar. The technique derives from Thailand, where it is called *laay rot nam*, or "design from washing". When only small areas are gold-leafed, positive designs are made by drawing sketches at the desired places, lacquer is placed on them, and then gold leaf. When they are almost dry, the gold leaf is washed off.

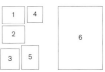

1 and 2. 19th-century lacquer of Victorian design made for Europeans, and household lacquer, black with red interior. Kyaukka, north of Monywa in the Chindwin District. Courtesy of Patrick and Claudia Robert.

3. Voluminous and imposing, this type of *hsun-ok* has recently captivated collectors. Most are made from woven matting and coiled bamboo, and many are clearly local in style. Courtesy of Patrick and Claudia Robert.

4. Victorian-influenced *yun* plate with green, yellow and black on a light red background. A royal family is depicted at the centre. Courtesy of Elephant House, Bangkok and Yangon.

5. *Hsun-ok* with an outstanding gold *kanot* (convoluted leaf) design on red, decorating the bowl and cover and red lacquer on the pedestal bases. Mon production, probably latter part of the 19th century. Courtesy of Patrick and Claudia Robert.

6. A representative collection of late 19th- and early 20th-century *yun* lacquer betel boxes. Incised designs appear extensively on cylindrical-shaped lacquer betel boxes. Betel leaves are placed at the bottom of the boxes. Above are two shallow trays: the lower one often contains dried tobacco and the upper, tiny containers of lime, sliced areca nut, cloves and other ingredients. These are all wrapped delicately in betel leaves to form a quid. The chewing of a betel quid, which gives one a lift is still popular in many sectors of the Burmese population. Courtesy of Elephant House, Bangkok and Yangon.

Shan Lacquerware

Since the Shan State is home to the trees from which the best lacquer is derived, some scholars consider that lacquerware production came to Bagan via Laikha. This is still the predominant centre of lacquerware production in the southern part of the state. Lesser centres are at Ywama and Tha-lei on Inle Lake. The most important centre in the north is Kengtung.

Rare wares whose main surfaces are covered with green lacquer are a notable product of the Shan State. The green is produced from a mixture of orpiment and indigo, both of which are found in the region. The orpiment is ground into a powder, and to it are added ground indigo, translucent gum, lacquer and resin. Green lacquer may be decorated with *yun*, *shwe-zawa* or *thayo* designs.

Red and black lacquer produced in the Shan State has a brilliant sheen. This may be due to the excellence of the lacquer in the region. These colours are often used in bold juxtaposition to create unusual designs. Many wares tend to be robust.

Kengtung is noted for the delicacy of hand-moulded gilded *thayo* work, particularly on rice baskets called *kotaute*, which have a black lacquer body, gilded *thayo* at the top, and panels below bearing figures of a couple from an ethnic group. These date to the period between the World Wars, and are now much coveted by collectors.

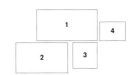

hsun-ok of varying designs.
2. Antique Shan lacquer house-hold wares with bold and often contrasting colours.
3. Antique Shan green lacquer wares with *yun* and *shwe-zawa* designs.
4. Extremely rare, antique open-work lacquer bowls.
All items from the collection of Patrick and Claudia Robert, except Plate 3, courtesy of the Elephant House, Bangkok and Yangon.

Plates 2–4 depict everyday items, whilst Plate 1 presents items for monastery use, all to designs from the Shan State.
1. Lacquerware for monastery use: hooded *daung-lan* (circular tray on a stand for serving meals) and

Relief-moulded Lacquerware

Relief-moulded lacquer (*thayo*) receptacles created mostly in Mandalay for Buddhist votive use, constitute an art form in which Myanmar excels. Lacquer is mixed with sifted paddy husk or cow dung ashes to which pulverized bone is added for strength, resulting in a plastic material easily moulded, modelled or stamped into relief designs. *Thayo* will adhere to wood, basketry, stone and metal. When each formed piece of *thayo* has hardened, it is lacquered at the rear and appropriately placed. *Thayo* designs may be inset with glass. Early glass was backed with mercury-treated foil, but in the latter part of the 19th century, mirror glass replaced it.

The most spectacular receptacles are the *hsun-ok*, tall pedestal-bowls used to offer food to monks. Their covers are surmounted by a pagoda-like finial at times inset with a *hintha* (Brahmani duck) or sphere. Monks' alms bowls (*thabeik*), covered and lavishly gilded and glass inlaid, are set on a *kalat*, a small tray with a stemmed base. *Kun-daung*, holders for betel leaves arranged in a spire as an offering, and betel boxes in the form of a *hintha*, are also popular votive objects of *thayo* decoration.

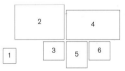

1. Victorian-inspired *thayo*-decorated *hsun-ok* and covered bowls from the Rakhine (Arakan) State.
2. *Hsun-ok* with spherical and *hintha* finials, *kalat* with a domed cover, covered monks' alms bowls placed on a *kalat*, and a gilded monk's fan. All from Mandalay.
3. Gilded *thayo*-decorated wooden *kalat* with elaborate aprons of *thayo*-decorated metal, one with a finialed pagoda-shaped spire, two with *thayo*-decorated *kundaung*, and another with a *thayo*-decorated water container and cup. From a nunnery at Sagaing.
4. Five *thayo*-decorated *hsun-ok* with glass insets, and a gilded *thayo* and black lacquer paddy container of Kengtung style.
5. Glass-inset gilded *thayo* table with legs of mythical animals including the *pyinsayupa* (a creature of five components, here elephant, lion, hoofed animal, serpent and fish).
6. Mon-produced glass-inset gilded *thayo* betel box of *hintha* shape. Table stand and betel box courtesy of Lopburi Arts and Antiques (Singapore). Other receptacles courtesy of Daw Myint Myint Sein.

Silver and Gold

The Burmese word for the finest silver is *baw*, and it is associated with the mines at Bawzaing and Bawdwin in the Shan State. Recent analysis has shown that at least by the 6th–8th centuries, silver from Bawzaing was used in Pyu coins. Fifth-century silver coins have been found in Rakhine State and in the Bago area. Of the same century are two finely wrought repoussé caskets from the Khin Ba mound, Thayekhittaya, with figures of the Buddha in low relief. Their sophistication suggests a long history of mining and silversmithing.

Inscriptions give evidence that in classical Bagan un-coined silver was employed as a means of exchange and in the production of votive objects. Rakhine kings minted coins from the 15th to 18th centuries. During the Konbaung period much of the silver was made from the at least 95% pure silver of the Bawdwin mine, from which very light, flexible silverware with restrained designs in low relief were created. With the colonial period, ornate high relief and lace-like repoussé came into fashion. Today, silversmithing continues in Sagaing District, Yangon, and at Ywama.

Old workings for gold have been found in Myanmar, and gold panning has gone on for centuries in the Irrawaddy, Chindwin and other rivers. Buddhist votive

objects and jewellery found in the Khin Ba mound attest to early and expert goldsmithing. The use of gold is often mentioned in Bagan inscriptions, and murals depict royalty with magnificent crowns and jewellery of gold. Foreign visitors at Bago in the 16th and Mrauk-U in the 17th century respectively, marvelled at the monarchy's wealth of gold and rubies. Bejewelled golden vessels and swords in the National Museum, Yangon, and other museums attest to the opulence of the Konbaung court.

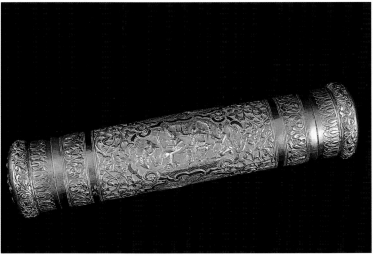

	2	5
1	3 4	6

1. Vessel and cover in the shape of a sacred bird, gold decorated with filigree work and inlaid with rubies and imitation emeralds, 19th century. Victoria and Albert Museum, London. Height 41.5 cm.
2. A collection of late 19th-century–early 20th-century repoussé-decorated boxes. Top left is a cigar box, and bottom right a match box cover. All the others are lime and betel boxes. Note the lace-like repoussé work on the specimen on middle right.
3. Silver embossed and engraved bowl with scenes from a *Jataka* story. Traditionally, bowls such as these would have been used as food offering bowls to the monks. A silver serving spoon would have been used to scoop and transfer rice from this bowl to the monks receiving alms.
4. A mid 19th-century official document carrier. The cylinder has two holes at each end for string to be passed through and knotted. It would have been slung across the shoulder of a messenger.

5. An elaborate table centrepiece, consisting of a round box and cover on a stand. Late 19th century–early 20th century. The engraving depicts small, lively figures from Burmese mythology–a gyrating *kinnara* (half human-half bird) and two fierce *bilu* (ogres).
6. A collection of silver-inlaid swords and knives. Courtesy of Daw Myint Myint Sein.
Plates 2–5 courtesy of Eastern Discoveries Antiques (Singapore).

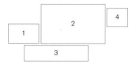

1. Double page from a *parabaik* illustrating protective *yantras* (geometric designs) and verses. Courtesy of Lopburi Arts and Antiques, Singapore.
2. Palm-leaf manuscript decorated with cinnabar and gilding, a specially woven binding ribbon (*sasigyo*) and a manuscript chest decorated with gilded lacquer relief inset with glass. Courtesy of Daw Myint Myint Sein.
3. Page from a *kammavaca*, lines of text in square letters of black lacquer. Second half of the 19th century–early 20th century.
4. A Buddhist monk at a monastery in Sa-le demonstrates how palm-leaf manuscripts are stored.

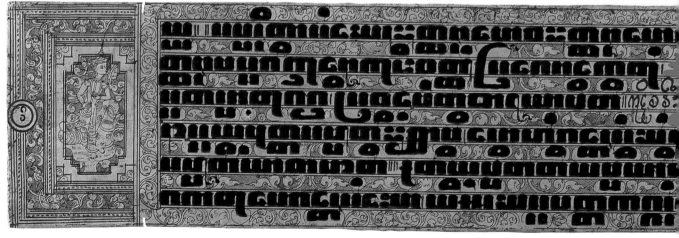

a scribe incised with a stylus horizontal lines from Buddhist texts, plus other treatises. Only rarely were diagrams or drawings inscribed. The leaves were rubbed with oil, earth and soot to preserve them and darken the script. Usually the title was inscribed on the cover while the donor's or author's name and the date appear at the end. The leaves, once collated, were placed between two boards to secure them; bamboo rods or string were passed through two holes bored at the centre. Size and decoration varied.

Kammavaca are volumes consisting of one, five or nine extracts from the Theravadin *Vinaya*, each relating to specific ceremonies associated with monks. Noel F Singer writes that the earliest *kammavaca* consisted of folios made of palm leaves, each of which had four lines of square-inked script on a gold or silver background ("Kammavaca Texts: Their Covers and Binding Ribbons", *Arts of Asia*, 23, May–June 1993). In the 17th century, folios began to be made of pieces of cloth coated with lacquer and painted with cinnabar, and the square letters were written in thick, black lacquer. On rare occasions, folios were of ivory. Designs in gilt which had been reserved for the ends of folios, end pages and wooden coverboards now began to appear between the lines of the text. By the second half of the 19th century, the lines of script on the folio increased to six or seven and sheets of brass or copper were introduced as folios.

Parabaik are manuscripts created from long strips of accordion-pleated paper processed from mulberry-tree bark. Those for everyday use were darkened with a powdered charcoal mixture. Markings made by steatite crayons could be erased and the paper re-used. *Parabaik*, coated with a chalk mixture and polished, often bear beautifully illustrated Buddhist and other texts and have covers of glass-inset *thayo*.

Manuscripts

The earliest manuscript found in Myanmar was in the 5th-century Khin Ba mound at Thayekhittaya. It is one inscribed with excerpts from the *Vinaya* and *Abhidhamma* (two of the three parts of the Pali *Tipitika*) on 20 gold leaves 16.5 cm in length and 4 cm in width. It had two gold covers bound together by a thick gold wire and its ends were fastened to the covers by sealing wax and small glass beads. Each leaf and cover had two holes through which the gold wire passed. This is stylistically related to two important manuscript types, palm-leaf manuscripts and *kammavaca*, both of which may have been produced early in the first millennium. The other important type, the *parabaik*, appears to date from the 14th century.

From at least the classical Bagan period (11th–13th centuries), specially processed leaves from the palmyra and talipot palms (*Borassus flabellifer* and *Corypha umbraculifera*) were employed as material on which

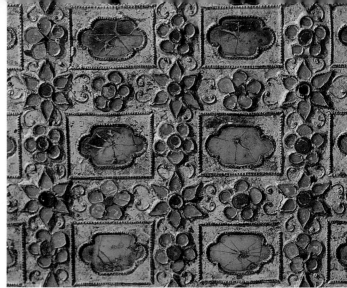

Scripture Chests and Cabinets

A library where Buddhist scriptural texts are kept is essential to every monastery. The texts are arranged in chests or cabinets called *sadaik*. The importance attached to these is expressed by the excellence of their craftsmanship. The body was constructed of wood, traditionally large single teak boards for strength and durability; it was often set on a high base to protect the texts from insects and damp, and was frequently covered with elaborate lacquer and inset glass decoration.

Most *sadaik* are in the form of long, rectangular chests, dovetailed at the joints and with a lift-up lid. The one *on right* is placed on a footed two level base. It is decorated with lacquer relief moulding covered with gold leaf and inset with glass, suggesting gemstones. Two rectangular panels enclose figures within ellipsoids. Between the latter are stemmed lotus buds and blossoms formed of inset coloured glass. The ellipsoids are echoed on the sides of the base.

Another type (*on left*) rises vertically in three levels and is influenced by European Victorian furniture. The two lower sections are for manuscripts; the top has a recess with a glass door to hold a Buddha image.

1. Decoration on a scripture cabinet emulating the gold and glass décor on the walls and doors of the Hmannandawgyi (Glass Palace), the most beautiful quarter of the Mandalay palace. The geometric design is formed of glass jewelled squares with a large bejewelled lotus at the centre of each.
2. Three-level cabinet of relief-moulded lacquer inset with glass and covered with gold leaf, with a place for a Buddha image. Courtesy of Daw Myint Myint Sein.
3. Scripture cabinet decoration consisting of relief-moulded lacquer and gold leaf with a wide border of convoluted lotus stems, buds and flowers, within which are rows of flowers and rectangular enclosed ellipsoids filled with glass.
4. Panel of a manuscript chest with a framed multi-coloured bird at the centre poised against a blue-green glass background overlaid with an arabesque of lotus foliage.
5. A rectangular chest with a border of glass inlaid in a geometrical pattern, enclosing a wooden framed panel with three arches on it which probably suggest the Three Jewels: Buddha, *Dhamma* and *Sangha*.
6. Imposing scripture chest on a two-level base featuring figures in ellipsoids, from Bagaya *kyaung*, Ava, early 20th century. All examples of decoration (except Plate 3 from Daw Myint Myint Sein's collection) courtesy of Patrick and Claudia Robert.

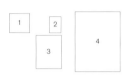

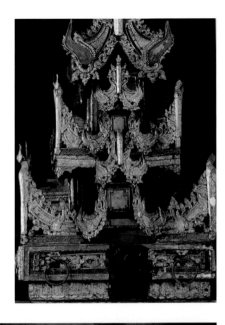

1. A gilded wooden pediment for a Buddhist shrine decorated with scrollwork and foliage, second half of the 19th century. Courtesy of Patrick and Claudia Robert.
2. A gilded wooden shrine for Buddha images inset with blue glass, from the Shan State. *Circa* late 19th century or early 20th century.
3. The abbot's gilded chair, the Nunnery, Sagaing, late 19th century or early 20th century.
4. The Lion Throne from the Mandalay palace, now in the National Museum, Yangon, 1857–1861.

Buddhist Altars and Thrones

Buddhist altars in Myanmar serve as places to which the faithful may come to revere the Buddha and express their joys as well as their anxieties. Thrones too, play an important role, since they represent both secular and spiritual authority.

In the design of the Lion Throne (*far right*) which dominated the audience hall of the Mandalay palace, artisans illustrated the concept that the Burmese monarch was the universal ruler in Buddhist cosmology and linked his throne to that of the *deva* Thagyamin's (Indra's) Tavatimsa realm. The pediment is decorated at the sides with *saing-baung* (flaring ornamental elements in the form of haunches of a wild ox). At its apex is the pinnacle of Mt Meru, the great mountain at the centre of the Buddhist universe. Above it is the Tavatimsa realm ruled by Thagyamin, on his throne in his palace. Beneath the pediment are ten-metre high sliding doors of gilt ironwork through which the king and queen would have passed to their seats. On either side are pilasters decorated at the top and the bottom with the figure of a *lokapala*, a guardian king of the universe. At the centre are roundels encircling a peacock and a rabbit, indicating the sun and the moon. Below in niches are small images of lions, from which the throne derived its name. These suggest that like the Buddha, to whom the lion is often equated, the monarch is strong and courageous.

An intricately carved preaching chair (*on right*) for the abbot of a monastery has a design at the top and sides similar to that on the Lion Throne. At the centre is a Wheel of the Law with eight circles suggesting the Noble Eightfold Path.

Textiles and Costumes

The peoples of Myanmar have a long history as accomplished textile weavers. Tang Chinese chroniclers noted that during the second half of the first millennium of this era, the Pyu, in what is now Central Myanmar, wore cloth of cotton. Murals, sculpture and glazed plaques from the late 11th century onwards depict a wide variety of textile designs and modes of dress.

The most distinctive weaving technique is a tapestry weave employing *lun-taya*, "one hundred shuttles" (but often about twice that) over and under warp threads to create weft *acheik* (wavy patterns). *Si* (tie-dyeing, literally "tying together, binding") is done by dyeing the thread in various colours to form a pattern and sealing them individually with bindings to safeguard the colours prior to dyeing the whole. The technique is usually employed in creating weft patterns but sometimes is used to make a design in the weft and warp simultaneously. Popular also is the supplementary weft technique whereby extra threads are woven into the weft to introduce patterns not in the basic design. Another technique, one derived from north-eastern Thailand and used in Ban-gauk (Bangkok) *longyis*, involves the use of two-tone, two-ply twisted silk threads in the warp to create a lustrous sheen and subtle patterns.

Most fabrics were and still are woven on a *yakan zin*, a large rectangular loom with a built-in seat for the weaver.

Fabrics are woven both for venerating the Buddha and the *Sangha* and for personal attire and home use. The former consists of the *ka-ba-lwe*, a bamboo-ribbed cloth for wrapping palm-leaf manuscripts; *sa-si-gyo*, ribbon to bind tightly the *ka-ba-lwe*; and *ticivara* (monks' robes of three pieces), plus shoulder straps for monks' alms bowls.

One of the delights of Myanmar is that the people continue to wear traditional dress. There have been some modern adaptations, but by and large Burmese attire remains its distinctive self.

1. The chosen formal wear fabric is *lun-taya acheik*. A status symbol, it is very expensive, labour intensive and time-consuming to make and was once limited to royal garments. The pattern is woven on the reverse side and is created from motifs developed over the centuries. An interplay of one or two colours is popular, such as a combination of pinks or blues.

This particular design incorporates three patterns: *nit sit lein kyo* (two twisted stripes), a variation on *taik kaung pan khet* (chief queen's floral garland) and *thoun gamoun ywet set* (Burmese number 3, *thoun*, joined with *gamoun*, creeper). Fabric courtesy of Patrick and Claudia Robert.
2. An unidentified seated lady wears a silk *hta-mein* (wrap-around skirt) and a Western-influenced *ein-gyi* (blouse or jacket); standing is a famous dancer, Sein Chit, wearing a plaid silk *hta-mein* and a *yin zin ein-gyi* (a jacket fastened down the front), *circa* 1910.

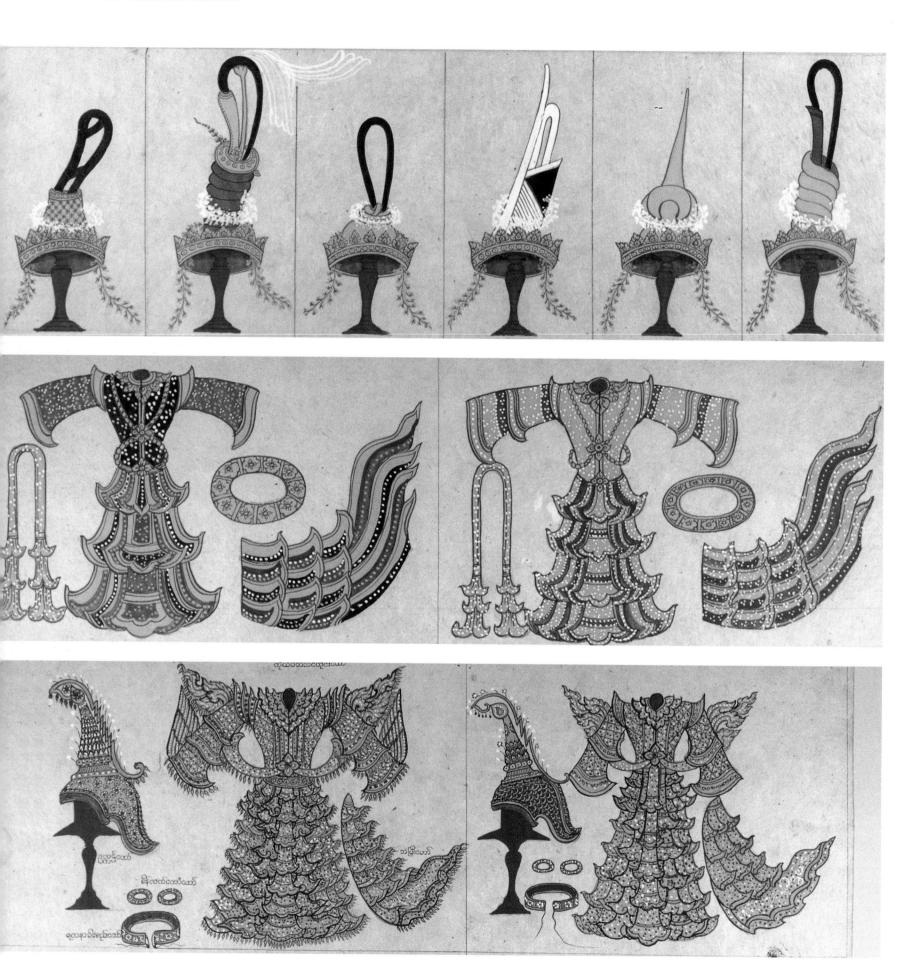

The Art of Adornment
Court Dresses

At the apex of the royal court was the king, regarded as the Universal Ruler. After him came the princes of the blood, among whom the heir apparent was paramount. First in rank of the four queens entitled to a palace was the South Queen, next the North, then the Middle, and last the West Queen. There were four lesser queens and junior queens and others rightly called concubines.

After royalty, came the king's ministers and generals, and lesser members of the court. All attire and the various accoutrements were controlled by strict and elaborate sumptuary laws. These were inscribed on *parabaik* or manuscripts, many of which remain today and may be viewed in museums, both in Myanmar and elsewhere.

Silk cloth brocaded with gold or silver flowers and animals could only be worn by royalty, ministers, and certain ministers' wives. The use of jewels and precious stones, so dear to every Burmese, was carefully regulated. Very few besides the king and his relatives could wear diamonds, rubies, emeralds and the like. Anklets of gold were strictly forbidden to all but the royal children. The decoration, metal, size and construction of spittoons, betel boxes, cups and so on were rigidly demarcated. Velvet sandals were worn only by persons of royal blood. Velvet and satin were imported, but velvet was woven in the Mandalay palace as well.

Also created there were special ceremonial robes for royalty made from *pazun-zi*, described by Adoniram Judson as "kinds of gold and silver lace" (*Judson's Burmese-English Dictionary*, 1853). These were heavy garments adorned with couched gold threads, sequins, gold, silver and gems. Cane was added at times for support.

The royal coronation regalia consisted of a nine-tiered white umbrella, crown, four-edged dagger, yak-tail fly whisk and slippers, all encrusted with gold and jewels. Other objects in the regalia were the *salwe*, gold or silver sashes worn as insignia of honour, rank or office. These consisted of chains clasped by brooches. The number of chains indicated rank; the king had 24. Also included were the royal long-stemmed fan, betel boxes, *laphet* (pickled tea) containers and many other items.

Ministers were subordinate only to the royal family. During times of war both they and princes of the royal blood might don the robes of a general; thus they had a right to both ceremonial ministerial robes and those of senior military officers.

Three 19th-century *parabaik* from the British Library, London, depicting:
1. Late Ava period coiffure of royal and high-ranking ladies, with hair pulled high through a golden diadem, stiffened and twisted into shapes deemed fashionable and suitable to the rank of the wearer.
2. Left, a *malliga* robe of black, green and red velvet incorporating a specially woven gold and silver lace-like cloth (*pazun-zi*), as worn by the chief queen, ornamented with gold and silver lace and flowers. Right, a *mahallata*, the chief queen's gem-studded robe of *pazun-zi* with green and red velvet. Wing-like attachable panels are shown with each garment.
3. Formal gem-ornamented ceremonial costumes of a princess, with *naga*-headed crown, jewelled belt, diamond bracelets, ruff and *dajin* (flame-like epaulettes), tiered sleeves and skirt and attachable wing-like panels.
4. King Thibaw (r. 1878–1885) and Queen Supayalat in full court attire. According to Henry Yule, the gold and jewel-encrusted costume of a Konbaung king actually weighed nearly 100 pounds; despite its brilliant evocation of wealth, status and power it was a daunting physical burden.
5. Royal robe of velvet with elaborate gold stitchery and kimono-like sleeves; dramatic wing-like panels project upward on each side at the bottom. Victoria and Albert Museum, London.
6. The dance of a young princess in ceremonial costume featuring a *naga*-headed crown, a *hta-mein* (wrap-around skirt) and velvet slippers.
Plates 4 and 6 from a private collection.

The ceremonial robes of ministers consisted of a long robe of velvet or satin having broad kimono-like sleeves and trimmed with gold braid and imported silk brocade. This they wore over a *pahso* (the lower garment worn by Burmese men) and at times an *ein-gyi* (jacket). Across the chest each proudly wore a *salwe* indicating his official rank. Cup-like jewelled ear plugs with long golden shafts thrust through the earlobes added to their splendour. The crowning glory was their *baung kaddiba*, a richly decorated velvet turban, with a broad band embellished with flowers of gold foil topped by a border of upright pointed gold leaves.

A general's formal attire was also worn over a *pahso*. Most important was the coat, consisting of a jacket with attached skirting. The sleeveless jacket was known as *myin-to*, and the full coat, *myin-shei*. Adorning the neck was a *ba-le-gwei*, a gorget with upswept wings. Below it on both the front and back were *ba-yek*, large medallions pendent from a necklace. Adding further dignity was a gilded broad-brimmed helmet (*shwe-pe kha-mauk*) which like a minister's headgear was decorated with a band of golden flowers and leaves combined to give a sense of height and strength. Underneath the helmet they wore a *paga-naga*, a wide band with flaps below to protect the cheeks and ears.

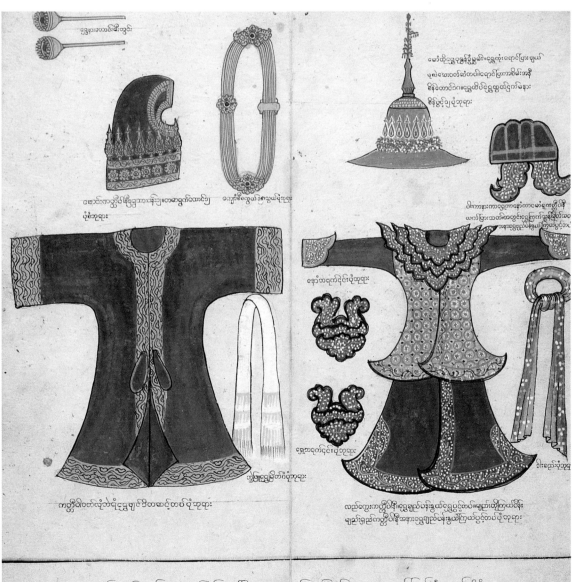

1. A Burmese prince wearing a general's uniform *circa* 1878.
2. *Baung-kaddiba* with gold foil flowers and vertical pointed leaves under a *fleur-de-lis*-like design.
3. Red velvet full-skirted *myin-shei* of a prince or minister with a golden *ba-le-gwei* and *ba-yek*.
4. Minister's robe with trim of imported gold brocade, worn over a red *pahso* with a supplementary weft design.
5. Minister wearing the robe in Plate 4 with a *salwe* across his chest, a mitre-like turban and a long-headed palm-leaf *yat* (fan), also an insignia of office.
6. Minister wearing a velvet robe and turban trimmed with gold, a white *ein-gyi*, and striped *pahso*.
7. Robes of a minister and general presented by the king to his purveyor, Saku Myosa Maha Min-Htin Sithu. On the left a red velvet robe with gold braid trim, gold-foil-trimmed turban, gold ear-plugs and *salwe*. On the right, a red

velvet *myin-shei* with *ba-le-gwei* and skirting ornamented with star diamonds and a jacket with gold embroidered flowers; *ba-yek* to be worn on the front and back; *shwe-pe kha-mauk*, here with colourful floral band and leaf decorations; *paga-naga* and waist-tie.
8. General with dress uniform over a *pahso* worn in pants fashion, followed by an attendant wearing his *pahso* tucked up about the waist, showing protective tattoos covering his legs above the knee.
9. Velvet *paga-naga* embroidered with gold florets, tendrils and stars. Plates 2, 3, 4 and 9 from the Victoria and Albert Museum, London; 1 and 5 from a private collection; 7 and 8 from the British Library, London; 6 courtesy of Lopburi Arts and Antiques (Singapore).

				6		8
1	3					9
2	4	5		7		

PRINCE AND HIS SERVANT.

The Art of Adornment
Post-Monarchy Apparel

During the Konbaung Dynasty (1752–1885) prior to the Mandalay period, women outside the court wore a *hta-mein* (a wrap-around skirt) in various ways. At times it was worn folded tightly across the abdomen slightly left centre of the waist. Murals indicate that when worn this way either no breast cover accompanied it or a *hpa-wa*, a shawl of considerable length and width, was used to cover the breasts. More often the *hta-mein* had a breast cloth attached at the top and the unit was folded tightly over the breasts to one side. Such apparel was called a *kha-tin-hto* or *yin-sha*. The breast cloth portion was often red, while the skirt was of lighter red with darker red horizontal stripes, or beige with brown and black and at times turquoise stripes. Both the *hta-mein* and *pahso* (a man's lower garment) were quite long and trailed on the ground.

The *pahso* were of the same material but were much wider, consisting of as much as two lengths of woven material. At times the ends were bunched at the front and tucked into the waist; at others they were pulled up between the legs to form long or short breeches. No jacket was worn on top, but sometimes a *hpa-wa*. A small flat *gaung-baung* (headgear or turban) with pseudo ear flaps and a stiff flame-like decoration on top was worn on formal occasions. By 1824, men's styles had changed somewhat as seen in the murals of the Pitakat-taik (manuscript library), Wet Kyi-in, Bagan.

Men wore a *pahso* with bold red or black grids on white, folded into short breeches to show their tattoed upper legs. While ordinary women continued to wear their customary attire, the wives of court officials wore a *hta-mein* with an unattached breast cloth called a *yin-khan* under a *htain mathein ein-gyi* (a hip-length jacket) of almost transparent muslin or cotton. Sir George Scott described in *The Burman: His Life and Nations* (1896) how the latter garment, surcoats and the like were reserved for officials by sumptuary laws. He described dress outside the Mandalay court as sombre. In that period women outside the court appear to have adopted a new form of dress. They wore a *hta-mein* of unobtrusive material with a black waistband and short train. An *ein-gyi* (a blouse or jacket) was worn on top. These basic designs were continued for more than two decades after the fall of the monarchy. Those who had money now dared to flaunt it by wearing heretofore forbidden silks, furs, jewellery and the *htain mathein ein-gyi*.

In the 20th century the *hta-mein* and *pahso* gave way to a more practical tubular garment called a *longyi*, worn by both men and women today, and a somewhat abbreviated *ein-gyi*.

Textiles

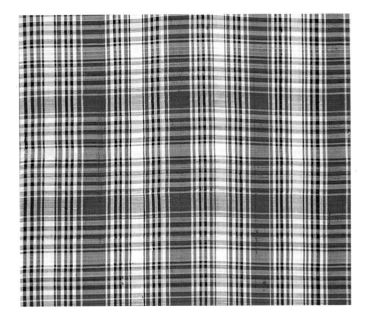

Cotton and silk were and are the chief materials used in the hand loom industry. Most of the former is imported from India and the latter from China. Natural dyes gave way to aniline in the 1880s.

Amarapura is the most important weaving centre and is known for its *lun-taya acheik* textiles woven by a technique said to have been introduced by weavers from Manipur captured by King Alaungpaya. Now weavers also produce imitations of traditional designs including those of the Kachin, Chin and other ethnic groups, some with rayon and nylon and highlighted by metallic threads.

Today, San Khan and Thapye Auk villages to the south produce cotton *si longyis* with weft twill weave designs. According to George W Bird in *Wanderings in Burma* (1897), Paleik in the Kyaukse area to the east was once a centre for silk production. Blankets and other home products are woven in the Monywa, Meiktila and Pakokku areas. Gangaw, known for its supplementary weave designs on brown and black silk and cotton, now mostly uses cotton. Shwedaung, north of Pyay (Prome), a centre for silk plaid production, presently has turned to making men's cotton plaid *longyis* while neaby Kyi Thei weaves cotton *longyis* with a warp and weft dyed design.

At Inle Lake in the Shan State, distinctive Shan women's *longyis* of red or green weft with warp-woven stripes are still produced. Woven principally by the Inthas, who came originally from Dawei (Tavoy), are *si longyis* with a weft twill design called Zimme (ie Chiang Mai) although no such textiles are known to have been made there. Further research is needed to establish the date when *si* production began at Inle, but in the 1930s Zimme *longyis* of red, burnt orange and sometimes green were popular, resembling Cambodian fabrics, especially those from Battambang. Later the designs and methods were modernized and new floral, pin stripes and other motifs were introduced.

Ban-gauk *longyis*, formerly woven in large numbers, are rarely made now due to the difficulty of the weave. A few cotton *longyis* are woven in Twante and Dawei, the latter formerly known for its small checked silk *longyis*. Rakhine (Arakan) State's popular men's cotton and silk *longyis* with supplementary weft remain in high demand and are imitated elsewhere. Supplementary weft designed fabrics continue to be produced in Sittwe, Thandwei, Kyaukpyu and Mrauk-U, Rakhine State.

1. Lady's shot silk *longyi* having a dark brown warp and a green weft with a supplementary weft floral design bearing a Kyaukse trademark on the upper part, pre-World War II, warp 184 cm, weft 104 cm.
2. Man's silk Ban-gauk *longyi* with geometric motif within a plaid pattern, Tha-lei village, Inle Lake, post World War II, warp 182 cm, weft 109 cm.
3. Lady's silk *longyi* with supplementary weft floral and striped motifs in silver and gold threads, Kyaukse, pre World War II, warp 204 cm, weft 108 cm.
4. Lady's cotton *longyi* with warp design in a band on the lower part of the *longyi*, Dawei, 1994, warp 174 cm, weft 112 cm. Note the similarity of the geometric motif to that in Plate 2, not unusual since the Intha weavers at Inle originated at Dawei.
5. Lady's cotton *longyi* with black supplementary weft design, Mrauk-U, 1995, warp 188 cm, weft 112 cm.
6. Man's cotton *longyi* with black supplementary weft diamond pattern, Sittwe, 1995, warp 188 cm, weft 112 cm.
7. Lady's silk *longyi* with tie-dyed warp and weft designs, Kyi Thei, *circa* mid-1930s, warp 172 cm, weft 104 cm.
8. Lady's silk Shan *longyi* with warp-woven stripes, *circa* mid 1930s, Inle Lake, warp 164 cm, weft 100 cm.
9. Lady's silk Zimme *si longyi* with weft twill floral design. The section to the left bearing vertical stripes is folded inside the front pleat and is not seen when worn. Impaw-khun village, Inle Lake, *circa* mid 1930s, warp 162 cm, weft 99 cm.
10. Man's *gaung-baung* of pink silk over a woven cane base, with its original box.
11. Lady's silk plaid *longyi*, Shwedaung, post World War II, warp 164 cm, weft 100 cm.
12. Lady's silk *lun-taya acheik longyi*, Amarapura, 1976, warp 168 cm, weft 100 cm.
All textiles are from a private collection, Bangkok.

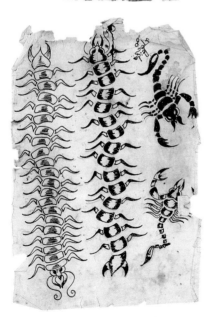

Tattoos

Traditionally, every young man in Myanmar would have been tattooed, not just on the upper body as is now the case, but very intensively from the knee to the waist. Tattoos were the mark of manhood and indicated bravery because the pain undergone was so great. In fact, in places such as the tender inside of the thigh and the knee joints, the pain could be unendurable and boys had to be given opium to relieve their distress.

Shans were considered the best of the itinerant tattoo masters. The designs were chosen from illustrations in palm-leaf manuscripts or on accordion-folded paper prepared from the bark of mulberry trees (*parabaik*). The designs were of actual or mythological beings: their power could confer physical invulnerability against all weapons, attract admiration and love, increase luck and charm, and enhance bodily beauty.

The tattoo master used a hollow brass instrument into which was fitted a pointed stylus with two or four vertical slots on the sides. The pigment was introduced into the slots; it was either vermilion, including various solutions according to magical requirements, which would fade away in time, or blue dye from lampblack, which was permanent. Fitted into the upper end of the brass tube was a bronze weight in the shape of a mythological being or *nat*, selected by the client.

The best masters first outlined the tattoo design on the skin with a brush, and then executed it with a series of punctures close together, forming what afterwards would fade into a rough line. The master held the puncturing instrument in his right hand and guided the point with the forefinger and thumb of his left, the hand resting firmly on the client's body. Each representation was surrounded by a roughly oval tracery of letters forming a frame. These letters conveyed a protective message. Grid patterns of squares bearing numbers in a manner offering protection, appeared in or around the basic figure tattooed.

With British colonization, the fashion of tattooing diminished, especially that on the lower part of the body. In the 1920s, the traditional method of tattooing gave way to less painful electrical means. Today, the implements used by the old masters have become collectors' items.

1–3. Contemporary tattoo designs including tigers, centipedes, scorpions and the like. Mandalay.

4. A tattooist's brass stylus (pointing upwards, showing the slits on the lower sides), a weight in image form, a box for a set of weights, and an accordion-pleated manuscript of black mulberry paper with tattoo designs. Items courtesy of Lopburi Arts and Antiques (Singapore).

5. Old postcard depicting a Burmese tattooist at work. Private collection.

6. Illustration from a *parabaik* of men with tattoos on the lower parts of their bodies. British Library, London.

7–10. Traditional tattoo designs; note the protective encircling letters and geometric grids. British Library, London.

Tattooing a Burman.

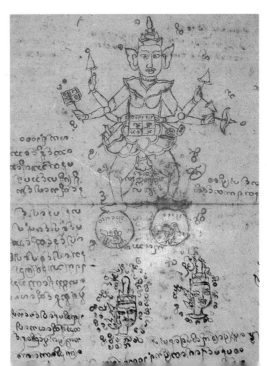

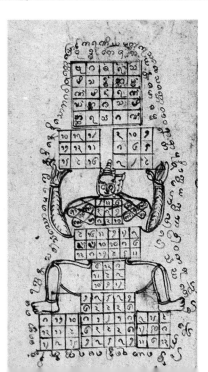

Embroidered Quilts (*Kalagas*)

Since the early 1970s, *kalagas*, colourful sequinned hangings with scenes from the life of the Buddha, *Jatakas*, and—to a lesser extent —secular themes, have been sought after by collectors worldwide. The term, meaning "Indian curtain" suggests an as yet undetermined Indian derivation. The art began in the mid-17th century and reached its zenith during the reign of King Mindon (1853–78) when the velvet which often forms the background was both imported and woven in the palace. The technique ("gold-thread stitching" in Burmese) involves appliqué, quilting and couching. Figures, foliage, architectural elements and so on, were cut from the materials—which include felt, flannel, cotton, silk, wool, lace and braid—and were attached to a background cloth of velvet or cotton, often with its own cotton backing. Sequins, imitation jewels and couched work in gold and silver thread created a rich appearance. Facial features were usually painted on.

Most early *kalagas* are in long rectangular form with stories illustrated in narrow strips. Architectural elements and foliage serve as scene dividers, and space is defined by the relative positioning of figures or by colours, for example, darker in front and lighter at the rear. Today, in the revived industry in Mandalay, *kalagas* of varying sizes and themes are made and their technique is used in the production of a variety of other goods as well.

1. Sequinned chariot with peacock inside. Names of donors given above. Courtesy of William Warren.
2. Sequential scenes from the Maha-ummagga *Jataka*. Note the *hintha* border motif. Second half of the 19th century.
3. Two scenes from the Life of the Buddha read right to left: Prince Siddhattha leaves the palace on horseback; Mara, the god of worldly pleasures, tries to deter the prince; Siddhattha cuts his long hair; his horse, heartbroken, dies. Second half of the 19th century. Plates 2 and 3 courtesy of Rama Art, Bangkok.

The Pagoda Alley Market

Religious life in Myanmar revolves around the *zeidi* or pagoda, the large, solid bell-shaped Buddhist monuments that pierce city skylines and dot the countryside throughout the nation. Many contain a small treasure trove of Buddhist relics: These may be materials thought to have been taken from the remains of the Buddha himself—typically bone, teeth or hair—or holy objects such as small Buddha images of varying materials, pieces of cloth blessed by venerated *sayadaws* (Buddhist masters) and gemstones.

A more visible cache of treasures can be found in the long, straight walkways radiating outward from the *zeidi* toward the four compass points. In the largest and most venerated pagodas and temples such as Shwedagon in Yangon, Mahamuni in Mandalay or Ananda in Bagan, these walkways have evolved over the centuries into sizeable enclosed passageways with vaulted ceilings. Vendor stalls lining the sides of such passageways carry on an ancient trade in Buddha images, prayer beads, temple souvenirs, folk art, monastic accoutrements, articles for home worship, and costumes for *pwe* (traditional Burmese theatre), *shin-pyu* (novitiation ceremony for boys), and *na-tha* (ear-boring ceremony for girls). Everyday items such as combs, mirrors, slippers, traditional medicines, cosmetics and books are also often available.

One of the alleys leading to the pagoda is often partially occupied by a section of astrologers and palmists who offer visitors the chance to have their past histories probed and their futures divined.

Religious worship, ceremonial preparations, grooming traditions, fortune-telling techniques—these are the practices of everyday Burmese life that set it apart from its neighbouring countries. In fact when we examine the aggregate of all that is offered in the great pagoda alley, it is clear that this is where the country's very *bamahsan-chin* or "Burmese-ness" is most visibly concentrated. A passage through a *zeidi* complex thus becomes in many ways a journey into the heart of Myanmar.

1	2

1. A collection of folk paintings on glass representing the *nats* (spirits). On sale in a pagoda alley market at Bagan, they are destined for the family shrine.
2. Herbal medicines and traditional cosmetics such as the ubiquitous *thanaka* powder are on sale at many pagoda alley markets.

paying respect to the *zeidis*, Buddhas and other holy images in a pagoda complex, the Burmese believe they can obtain a better future, whether in this life or the next.

Although foremost in importance, religion is only one of the components of *bamahsan-chin* inculcated via pagoda visits. Woven sarongs or *longyi* for both men and women, simple velvet thong slippers, cosmetics and traditional Burmese medicine—all found in abundance in large pagoda complexes—add significant dimensions to the Burmese cultural identity. Very seldom does one see imported goods for sale at pagoda stalls, as such products are relegated to more secular markets. Thus any visit to a *mahazeidi* or great pagoda ultimately functions as a reaffirmation of the Burmese identity.

Buddhism as practiced in Myanmar mandates no particular "Sabbath" or day of the week when the Burmese must visit their pagodas. Instead it is the practice of the Burmese—alone, with friends, or with family members—to enter a pagoda complex whenever they feel the need to create *kutho* or "merit" (from the Pali *kusala* or "wholesome"). Particularly auspicious days to make merit include the full and new moon phases of the 28-day lunar month, on one's birthday, or whenever a little spiritual help from the Buddhist cosmos is desired.

Many of the objects found for sale in the great pagoda alley markets have been designed as offerings to be presented at small altars surrounding the *zeidi*. Most commonly these include candles, flowers, incense and small *hti* made from paper disks attached to bamboo strips, parasol-style. Through

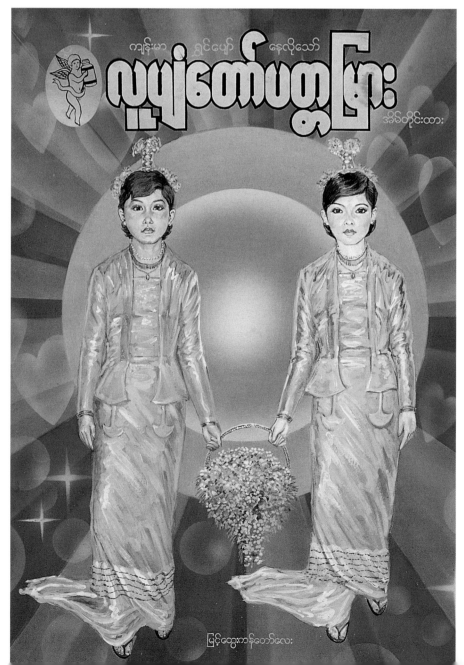

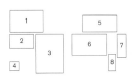

4. Slippers to be worn by novitiates during the *shin-pyu*.
5. A typical pagoda alley, lined with vendors. Monks, the devout and people simply going shopping are frequent visitors.
6. A shop selling Buddha images. In the background is a replica of the most revered image in Myanmar–the Mahamuni Buddha image. The stall-owner fashions some gilting in the foreground.
7 and 8. Intricately decorated hats to be worn by performers during the *pwe* dance-drama.

1. A family strolls through a pagoda alley on the way to a novitiation ceremony.
2. Fashioning *hti*–umbrella-like ornamentation to be mounted atop the *zeidi*.
3. A label from one of Myanmar's most popular tonics.

Shops for Religious Objects

Virtually every Burmese household features one or more altars where the tenants pay respect to Buddhism and to the spirit world. Lacquered and gilded wooden platforms of varying sizes, placed on high tables or fastened to the wall well above waist level, support religious figures of the family's choice. The highest altar-top is reserved for Buddha images, while *nat* figures are confined to lower altars in a separate area of the room—or even in a separate room altogether.

These altars, along with the images of the Buddha and various favoured *nat* figures, are most likely bought from one of the many shops lining the alleys leading to the pagoda. In addition to the traditional altar tables and altar cases, gilded cane baskets may also be purchased. These are hung from a pillar, rafter or roof beam somewhere in the house and usually contain a large, unhusked coconut—an offering to the house guardian *nat*, Eindwin Min Mahagiri.

Although it may appear to outsiders to be a conflict between Buddhism and *nat* worship, the Burmese merely divide their devotions and offerings according to the two respective spheres of influence: Buddha for future lives, and the *nats* for problems in this life.

1. A shop containing many of the requisites for home worship of Buddha, Buddhist *bodhisattvas* and *nats*.
2 and 3. Two pairs of eyes for the reconstruction of broken images and for repairs to the *singha* lion.
4. These ornate white umbrellas are used to shade holy images whenever they are moved in a procession. During the *shin-pyu* they may also be held over the head of white-robed novitiates.

Religious Offerings' Stalls

In the average pagoda alley, a preponderance of the merchandise offered for sale consists of an affordable assortment of goods which worshippers can purchase for use as temple offerings. Such materials may be reverently placed before any of the numerous Buddhist altars found within a temple or pagoda compound, from the smaller astrologically oriented "planet" shrines to the pagoda's principal Buddha image.

Many temple-goers believe that the quantity of *kutho* or spiritual merit that naturally accumulates in one's life may be enhanced by making regular offerings of this kind. In the minds of many there is a direct numerical relationship between the amount of money spent to purchase offerings and the amount of *kutho* acquired.

Such donations may also be made in conjunction with specific needs or requests, or to overcome perceived obstacles in one's daily life. In this respect it is believed that the Buddha may grant a wish or solve a problem in return for having received an offering. Whether performed for the acquisition of merit or for the petitioning effect of prayer, the essential propitiatory nature of such acts is one of the pagoda's main reasons for existence.

1 and 3. Small *hti* made of bamboo strips and topped with coloured paper cut into umbrella-like shapes are the most inexpensive and popular of pagoda offerings. Often a pagoda astrologer will recommend the size, number, and colour of *hti* to be purchased by his clients and offered to the shrines. The umbrella motif symbolizes the supportive-protective relationship between the worshipper and the Buddhist religion; the donor supports the pagoda and the religion in return protects the donor.
2, 4 and 5. An artisan/vendor fashions "flowers" consisting of folded *kyat* notes for monastery offerings. The money is used for the maintenance of the shrines and other religious structures, or for the construction of new ones.
6. Other formats for making monetary donations include bills folded into the shape of Mount Meru, the mythical centre of the Buddhist cosmos, and others fitted together in the shape of a banyan tree (*Ficus religiosa*) leaf. This leaf symbolizes the culminating episode in the Buddha's religious journey, in which he sat at the foot of a banyan and vowed not to leave until he had attained enlightenment.

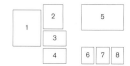

1. A *nat kaun*. Typically a *nat kaun* consists of a small wooden enclosure with a peaked roof, containing an image of the *nat* in worship. It can vary in size from a small altar-like wall attachment in the home, to a mini-house on stilts outdoors. Offerings are placed in front of the *nat* image.

2. Among the most famous of the 37-*nat* pantheon are the Taungbyon brothers, said to have been warriors in King Anawratha's 11th-century army. They were executed for failing to lay bricks at a pagoda as ordered. The appropriate offerings for the older brother, Shwe Hpyin Gyi, are soft drinks, while Shwe Hpyin Nge prefers liquor and fried chicken.

3. The Taungbyon brothers flank their mother, Mei Wunna. She is one of the most important Mt Popa *nats* because of her power to aid devotees in all religious endeavours, including the construction of pagodas. In the background stands a realistic rendering of Mt Popa.

4. The *nat* family of U Tint Te, his wife Shwe Nabe and their daughter Ma Hne Lay, guardians of the home and family, in a shrine at Mt Popa.

5. Myin Hpyu Shin, astride a white horse (upper left) watches over villages, quarters, wards and neighbourhoods. The smaller figure in front of Myin Hpyu Shin is U Min Kyaw, commonly known as Ko Gyi Kyaw. He bestows prosperity upon his followers in return for offerings of liquor. Ko Gyi Kyaw is a favourite subject of *nat pwes*, in which spirit mediums enter into trance in the hope of being temporarily possessed by his raucous spirit.

6, 7 and 8. Colour posters on sale in a Mandalay market. They may be used at a home shrine in lieu of figures, and depict: (on left) Shan brother and sister, Komyo Shin and Pule Yin, protectors of travellers who offer them pickled tea and sticky rice to the sound of a Shan gong; (middle) half human, half buffalo, Nankaraing Mei Daw, who protects devotees by destroying enemies when offered fried fish; (right) Sawgadaw, Yawgadaw, Nawgadaw and Seigadaw who represent the four compass points. Skilled in the weaving of magical spells and hexes, they must be offered uncooked chicken giblets in late evening by candlelight.

Spirit Shrines and *Nat* Images' Shops

During the 12th century the widespread adoption of Buddhism suppressed, but never replaced, the pre-Buddhist practice of *nat* (spirit) worship. *Nat* worship dates back to proto- and possibly pre-historic times; originally, it revolved around land, sky and water spirits, and was obviously linked to agricultural endeavours. But by the Bagan era, historical personages started gaining spirit status, probably in response to increased centralization of governing power (giving people martyrs to pay tribute to), and possibly influenced by similar cults in India.

Many *nats* are thought to be descended from people who had died violent, unjust deaths. These supra-human *nats*, when correctly propitiated, can aid worshippers in

accomplishing important tasks. The most potent of the *nats* make up a well known pantheon of 37, all of whom make Mt Popa their main spiritual abode. Today, this rock outcropping jutting from the plain near Bagan remains a major point of pilgrimage for many Burmese.

A visit to a temple reveals any number of *nats* housed in shrines dotted around the temple compound, in apparent contrast with the Buddhist nature of the place. And on sale in the pagoda alley markets are all the figures in the 37-*nat* pantheon—and more. These are purchased by the devout, and when placed in *nat kaun* (spirit home) shrines in the home, become the recipients of food, liquor, flowers and other consumables. Thus are the powerful spirits placated.

Monks' Outfitters

Buddhist males in Myanmar are expected to shave their heads and temporarily don the robes of the *Sangha* or monkhood at least once in their lives. Many enter the *Sangha* twice, first as a *samanera* or novice monk in their pre-teen years and again as a *pongyi* or fully ordained monk some time after the age of 20. A novice keeps ten monastic vows and typically spends an auspicious nine days in robes (those from impoverished families may stay longer), while a *pongyi* follows 227 vows and is expected to stay in robes for up to three months. The optimum interval for the latter is Waso, the "Buddhist Rains Retreat" season extending from July to October.

Typically, every monk is given the eight requisites permitted by the millennium-old Theravada Buddhist *Vinaya* or monastic code: Robe set (consisting of a lower cloth, an upper cloth, and an outer cloth), waistband, alms-bowl, razor, water strainer (for filtering insects from drinking water) and sewing thread for robe repairs. These will be obtained from a specialist shop in the pagoda alley, and donated to a monk by those seeking merit.

In addition to accruing spiritual merit for themselves and for their families, these short-term monastic sojourns form a very important part of a Burmese man's cultural and literary education.

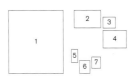

1. **Specialist shops such as this one in Mandalay stock the various articles of clothing and personal implements required in Buddhist monastic life. Myanmar's Buddhist laity may purchase these items and present them to the *pongyi kyaung* or monastery during religious festivals, or at any time they wish to prove their devotion to Buddhism.**
2. **In addition to the eight basic requisites prescribed for the *pongyi*, a certain number of additional articles may be kept and used. These include the leaf-shaped fan (for modestly hiding the face during public chanting sessions as well as for self-cooling), rosary beads, umbrella, sandals and small aluminium tiffin cariers for collecting "messy" foods such as soups or**

curries during the morning alms round.
3. **Although basically nothing more than large rectangular pieces of cloth, monks' robes come in a variety of fabrics, colours and stitching styles. Novices tend to wear brighter colours than older monks, for example, and heavier robes may be used during cooler months.**
4. **Robes, waistband, alms-bowl, strainer, razor, and sewing thread, the eight requisites for the *Sangha*. These items may be purchased from a shop in the pagoda alley as a merit-making exercise. Each dawn, monks walk in single file from household to household near their monasteries with the black lacquer bowls, collecting morsels of food for their daily sustenance.**
5 and 6. **A rosary and a fan, inscribed with tenets of *Abhidhamma* or Buddhist philosophical doctrine. The more expensive rosaries are made of *ahmwe daing* or sandalwood.**
7. **A wrapper for a set of monastic robes.**

Vendors of Alabaster Buddha Images

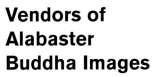

Burmese artisans craft Buddha images from a variety of materials, including wood, stone, bronze, iron and jade, but it is the alabaster figure that most captures the fancy of the average person in Myanmar. Today, row after row of these pure-white, serene-faced statues may be seen in many of the shops lining the pagoda alley.

Virtually all of the alabaster used for Buddhist sculpture in Myanmar comes from quarries at Sagyain, about two hours north of Mandalay by road on the way to Mogok. Quarry operators or alabaster wholesalers transport huge chunks by truck to Mandalay, where they are purchased by workshops clustered near the highly revered Mahamuni Pagoda.

Particularly in the region around Mandalay, Buddhists equate the white translucence of the milky marble with religious purity. The smooth white surface also makes an excellent canvas on which to apply gilt or painted detail.

1. Figures such as this heavily adorned Buddha image would originally have been bought from an alabaster Buddha vendor. The decoration would have been added afterwards, but before the image was placed in a temple. thus, the donor would accrue merit.

2. A gallery of Buddhas, all in the classic *bhumisparsa* (earth-touching) pose, await purchasers.

3. Artisans carve three classes of Buddha images, ranked by quality and detail of workmanship. First-class figures are usually sculpted by special order only and may take weeks to complete.

4. A sculptor applies the finishing touches to a small Buddha figure. Hanging overhead are iron umbrellas or *hti*, used to top *zeidi* spires.

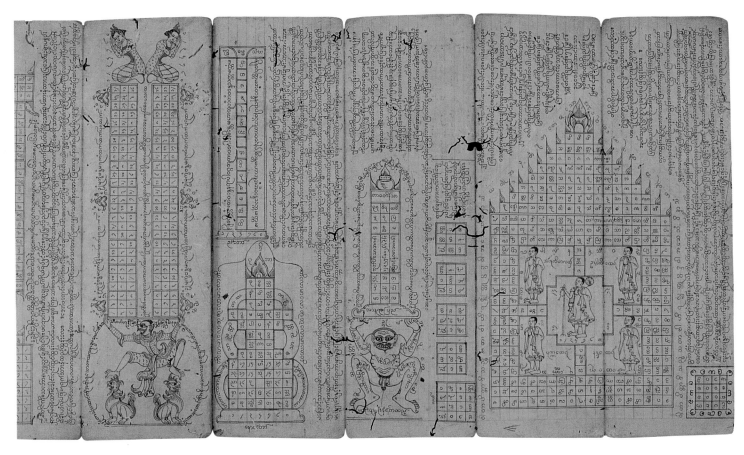

Astrologers and Palmists

When found in a pagoda alley, an astrologer's parlour will usually occupy a special section alongside other such parlours; fortune-tellers, palmists and astrologers all vie for business side by side. They are frequently consulted by the Burmese who consider that the position of the stars and planets have a great influence on one's life.

Most Burmese parents try to hire an astrologer to create a natal chart or *zatar* shortly after the birth of a child. Traditionally, these were inscribed onto palm leaves or bamboo slats, but nowadays more every-day materials such as cardboard may suffice. Each *zatar* contains a record of one's birth date and time along with the relative positions of the planets of the Indian zodiac at birth. The Burmese keep the *zatar* in a safe place in the home so that it can be re-examined by an astrologer whenever it is necessary to divine the auspicious time and date for weddings, funerals and even commercial negotiations.

Most Burmese palmists follow the Cheiro method, named after the famous 19th-century Egyptian palmist who said "A face may lie, but a hand will never".

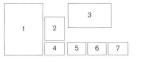

**1. One of the many astrologer's parlours along the entrance to the Mahamuni pagoda, Mandalay.
2. Palmistry ranks with astrology as one of the most important services in the pagoda alley.
3. A treatise on astrology. Courtesy of Lopburi Arts and Antiques (Singapore).
4, 5 and 6. A palmist examines the natal chart and palms–right hand for the future, left hand for the past–of a visitor.
7. The *zatar*, folded and bound with string to protect it.**

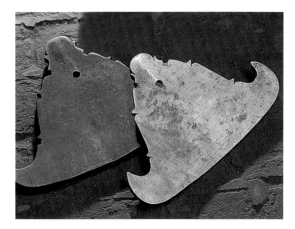

	5
1	
2	6
3 4	

Vendors of Bells and Gongs

It is not only in temple compounds and monasteries that one finds bells and gongs in Myanmar. Many Burmese will also display these items—usually bought from a specialist vendor in the pagoda alley—in their homes. They are considered items of devotion.

The classic designs for Burmese bells and gongs date back many centuries to an era when clocks had yet to be introduced. In today's Buddhist monasteries, time is still measured by the sound of padded hammers striking bronze surfaces: calling the monks to chanting sessions or meditation; announcing alms rounds or meal times; starting classes in *Dhamma* (Buddhist philosophy).

Certain gongs and bells are struck freely by visitors to shrines and pagodas as a form of prayer, homage or supplication. The round, flat gong of Shan origins produces sharp tones that are a favourite of *nat* worshippers; the large, ornate and more mellow-sounding temple bell is sounded three times by Buddhists paying tribute to the Buddha, the *Dhamma* and the *Sangha* (monastic community).

1. The flat, double-flanged *kyeyzi*, the holiest of Burmese bells, is used in conjunction with meditation, chanting, funerals and the collection of temple donations.
2. Shan gongs feature heavily in *nat pwe*, dances performed to invite spirit possession.
3 and 4. These temple bell frames are consigned to planet shrines within a temple compound: the dragon design for Saturday-born and the rat design for Thursday-born worshippers.
5. Stacks of cymbals have been placed before a family shrine to Thurathati (Saraswati in Sanskrit), the Hindu goddess of education and music.
6. A sonorous collection of bells, gongs and *kyeyzi* on sale in a shop in a pagoda alley.

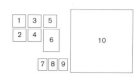

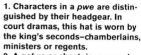

1. Characters in a *pwe* are distinguished by their headgear. In court dramas, this hat is worn by the king's seconds—chamberlains, ministers or regents.
2. A *salwe* or chestpiece worn by male novitiates.
3. The dragon headdress signifies the *naga meidaw* (she-dragon *nat*).
4. A *belu-ma* (ogress) wears a ferocious green mask.
5. The *ponna* (Brahmin astrologer) who wears this hat feeds malicious gossip to the heroic king in a *zat pwe* (dance-drama based on *Jataka* stories) stirring up trouble and quickly becoming the set villain.
6. Buffalo masks symbolize Nankaraing, a half-woman, half-bovine *nat* of Mon origins.
7, 8 and 9. These *shin-pyu* invitations depict the young Prince Siddhattha leaving the palace and renouncing his royal status to begin the long journey toward Buddhahood—a metamorphosis symbolically encapsulated in the novitiation ceremonies.
10. The mock royal accoutrements, necessary for both the *shin-pyu* and the *na-tha* ceremonies, on sale at a specialist outfitters.

Ceremonial Costumiers (*Shin-pyu*, *Na-tha* and *Pwe* Dresses)

Almost all boys between the ages of five and 15 participate in the *shin-pyu* or novitiation ceremony, during which sons take up the robe and bowl of Buddhist monasticism for a few days to earn religious merit for their parents and confirm their status as Buddhists. Girls of a comparable age may undergo a similar rite of passage known as the *na-tha*, during which their ears are pierced and they receive religious instruction from a Buddhist abbot.

In a procession from the family home to a temporary ceremonial hall near a monastery where the novitiation takes place, boys usually ride on ponies while girls sit in bullock carts. For both the *shin-pyu* and the *na-tha*, boys and girls are dressed in mock royal accoutrements, including heavily sequinned crowns, elaborate gold-threaded tunics and special slippers. All these are available from specialist shops in the pagoda alley. When enough money is available, a *pwe*—a live variety performance involving music, dance and comedy—may be hosted the night before a novitiation to celebrate the event and receive the *nats*' blessings.

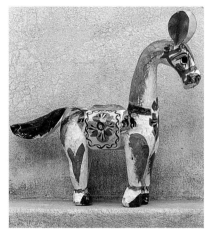

Toy Shops

Miniature animal figures, autos and drums seem to have a universal appeal for children everywhere, and the children of Myanmar are no exception. From a child's point of view, part of the fun of a visit to a religious site may be the possibility of buying a toy. Numerous vendors along the pagoda alleys stock a large array of brightly coloured toys.

While religious art such as Buddhist sculpture and the crafting of articles for *nat* worship require an adherence to relatively strict iconographic formulae, everyday folk art allows ample room for whimsy and innovation. In addition to toys, figures from Burmese mythic theatre, such as the *thu-nge-daw* or page boy/court messenger, are available. Some of the objects occasionally offer cultural symbolism too.

Sagaing has been a major centre for the crafting of toys for four generations. Inexpensive techniques involving the application of *papier mâché* to bamboo frames reduce the retail cost of such art to a level almost anyone can afford. In a process that takes about three days, the toys are fashioned from strips of paper soaked in rice paste and moulded around clay or wooden forms. Once the *papier mâché* dries, the figures are painted or gilded.

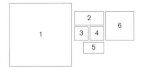

3, 4 and 5. Animal figures, which double up as toys for children. Spring-mounted heads add an extra touch of realism and movement to animal figures.
6. A *thu-nge-daw* or page boy. This individual carries communiqués to and from the royal characters in classical dance drama as well as marionette theatre. Always portrayed as a positive and energetic personage, he thus presents a cultural role model for children growing up in Myanmar.

1. A pagoda vendor's display of folk art and toys. The large black-eyed figures represent the auspicious *zee-kwet* or owl, to be displayed in pairs near the front of a shop to summon business success.
2. Bullock cart.

Marionette Vendors

Marionette theatre or *yok-thei pwe* enjoyed a pre-eminent place in Myanmar's performing arts tradition in the 18th and 19th centuries. The movements created by master puppeteers using the colourfully garbed and carefully assembled jointed wooden puppets in fact influenced the development of *zat pwe*, dance-drama later performed by live actors. Even today Burmese classical dance shows a pronounced similarity to marionette movements.

As in *zat pwe*, the primary subject matter for Burmese marionette theatre comes from the *Jatakas*. Favourite tales include those stories which emphasize royal court intrigue and provide moral instruction via the performance's subtext.

Standing up to a metre high, the marionettes may be manipulated by a dozen or more strings. Some of the older, more elaborate figures, particularly those representing *nat* or spirit roles, display as many as 60 strings attached to every moveable part of the puppet, from elbows to eyebrows. A *yok-thei* performance displays not only the talents of the puppeteers, but of the singers, musicians, woodcarvers, embroiderers and set designers as well.

Due to the breakdown of royally sponsored classical arts during the British colonial era and the advent of motion pictures, *yok-thei pwe* declined by the 1930s. It is now mostly relegated to performances held for foreign tourists. The puppets themselves, however, are still extremely popular. They are often purchased by Burmese and tourists as souvenirs or gifts and feature prominently in almost every shop in the great pagoda alley market.

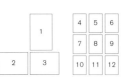

1. Puppeteers at work.
2 and 3. Design motifs used in the *kalaga* and marionette costumes reflected 19th-century court dress. Nowadays, the embroidery techniques used for the *kalaga* have joined the repertoire of costuming options for souvenir marionettes.
4. Marionettes are carved and fitted together such that most of the basic human movements involved in walking, dancing, and gesturing may be imitated. Older, pre-1970 puppets are more versatile than those created for the tourist market.
5–12. A traditional *yok-thei* troupe will consist of 28 puppet roles. These comprise: Thagyamin ("king of the gods"); a king, queen, prince and princess; a regent; two court pages; an old man and an old woman; a villain; a hermit sage; four royal ministers; two clowns; one good and one evil *nat*; a Brahmin astrologer; an ogre; a *zawgyi* (alchemist); a horse; a monkey; a *makara* or mythical sea serpent; and an elephant. Pictured here are (5.) two ogres, (6.) a horse, (7.) a queen, (8.) a prince, (9.) a comedian or clown, (10.) an old man, (11.) a king and (12.) a *zawgyi* or alchemist. Overleaf. The costumes of the prince (standing) and comedian (seated) in traditional folk theatre or *a-nyeint pwe* are identical to those used in marionette theatre. Both types of performance bring together the collective skill and inspiration of singers, musicians, comic improvisers, costume-makers, and set designers.

Index